BOLT

FROM

THE

BLUE

ELAINE C STONE

BOLT FROM THE BLUE

43 Minutes of Death And the Journey Back

ELAINE C. STONE

Copyright © 2024 by Elaine C Stone

All rights reserved.

Printed in the United States of America.

No part of this publication may be reproduced, distributed, or transmitted in any form or by any means, including photocopying, recording, or other electronic or mechanical methods, without the prior written permission of the publisher, except as permitted by U.S. copyright law. For permission requests, contact [include publisher/author contact info].

For privacy reasons, some names, locations, and dates may have been changed.

ISBN: 979-8-9905256-0-3

Library of Congress Control Number: 2024908318

Visit the author's website at www.elainestone.net

Book Cover by Ethan Unzicker

Editor: Ayessha Paarkar (Fiver@Ayessha P)

First Edition 2024

Published by Elaine C Stone

Ruther Glen, Virginia 22546

www.elainestone.net   www.facebook.com/elaine.c.stone

boltfromthebluebook@gmail.com

DEDICATIONS

To Jonathan,

Your winsome nature and stealth sense of humor kept me engaged, filling me with admiration at every turn. You laid your heart open: giving many private details to this project, hoping to honor God and help someone else on their journey. You carry physical marks of amazement/miracles, but also inward-ones, making you remarkable to the core. Your story lives inside of me like a dear friend; a cherished gift.

To the Colson Family,

You tirelessly opened yourselves to sharing the most difficult moments life presents. Through tears and triggers with authenticity you persevered in telling; touching me deeply. Thank you for trusting me with your most inward thoughts and devastating heartbreaks. I am humbled and honored. Your recollections have changed me; deepened my faith, inspired my soul.

To my Husband, Family, and Friends,

You cheered me on to complete this task, praying for the countless ways I was challenged. My "dear ones" who never tired of me saying for the thousandth time, "I've got to finish this book!" (Which was on every "to do" list for the past eight years.) You all knew I didn't know what I was doing, but believed I could. You supported beyond reason. I love you and adore the way you love me!

To My God,

"How could you entrust me with something so sacred when you knew I didn't have any idea how to write or complete a book?"

I am flattened that you would. The way you brought Jonathan back to life spurred me on in belief. I believe you have purpose in putting this story to pages.

I'm overwhelmed with gratitude for how you supported me during the darkest moments of this writing process. An avalanche of personal trauma and grief flooded me while penning this book, but I never got your release to quit. Instead, you spoke love, life and comfort into my soul; giving me strength to take the next step.

Even though I have never seen your face, your goodness, handprints, and earthly interventions fill the telling of this true story; revealing your heart and swelling mine.

May these words testify to your glory, greatness, unexplainable ways, and love.

All to Your Glory.

Introduction

June 3, 2009.

Sitting in my usual Wednesday night church spot, right side under the balcony, our Children's Pastor was speaking. Abruptly interrupting, an emphatic haunting female voice echoes from the Balcony.

"Does ANY ONE KNOW where Lavonne M. is?"

"My son has been struck by lightning and I need to get to the hospital!!"

"I need to give her my children!!!"

A loud ghostly desperate cry from a mother with an injured young. My stomach sank immediately. You don't forget moments like this, chilling to the bone! Everything stood still and silent, someone spoke up. I think our Pastor said, "Lavonne are you in here? Does anyone know where she is?" "Will someone help her please?" Several darted into action.

Turns out Lavonne had left church, but others in the foyer assisted Judy Colson, that evening. Taking care of her children, through other connections, so she was free to go to the hospital.

That was my introduction to the Colson family.

My husband and others visited the Emergency Room later. We were on the fringe of this experience. Over the years, we heard bits of the story unfold, running into the family once at a restaurant. I didn't know what they looked like, but my husband has a keen memory for "people" details.

I never dreamed I would one day be spending years crafting their story to share with others. Through Lavonne, about a year after the accident, I was approached about helping them write a book. I had my plate full of other assignments, so I declined. Five years later, my husband ran into Judy and asked if a book had ever been written. She said, "no", that plans fell apart.

Upon his suggestion, she called me again. We met and I prayed. I knew this was my assignment. Writing articles, short stories, Bible studies, and columns spanned my writing career, so to take on a book, a "memoir/biography" of sorts, was way beyond my comfort zone. Yet, I knew I was supposed to.

Judy said something to me, which rings in my ears and heart, "Everyone who told our story — Doctors, Therapists, Newspaper, TV news stations, etc. — always leave God out of our story!

"WE WANT GOD IN OUR STORY!"

Those words, too, chilled me to the bone, and haunted me. Still do!

I began this journey reading medical files, then I interviewed family members at great length, read press releases, watched videos, went to a few events. All of this to bring an accurate vision of what happened, so that you, the reader, might have a front row seat to these unbelievably stunning events.

What the Colsons have lived through is remarkable, unexplainable, noteworthy, and divine. God's fingerprints, handprints, and heart is all over their story. There is something in this story that every human alive can relate to. Their sorrows and struggles are enormous, but so are their joys and victories.

I hope by sharing Jonathan's story, each person will leave these pages enhanced, encouraged, inspired and hopeful. This was not an ordinary event with expected outcomes. This was an extraordinary one-in-million happenin: With the expected outcome being death.

But, God ...

You can predict lots of things in life or even mathematically figure out probabilities. But when you add God into an equation, you will never be able to explain or predict the outcome. His ways are not our ways and His mind, beyond our comprehension.

I hope you find God on these pages and marvel, as we do, at what he has done. The Colsons' desire to share their story is so many of you will find encouragement in the very hardest places life takes you. We can not answer the millions of questions these scenarios raise.

But, we can answer The Who and The How!

Who? God

How? By His Miraculous Interventions

Contents

1. The World Went White! — 1
2. Mary Washington Hospital — 6
3. Before The Bolt ... Childhood & Elementary Years — 10
4. White FLASH! Blinded! — 20
5. Bolt from the Night — 32
6. Medical College of Virginia (MCV) — 40
7. 2nd Movie Memory — 56
8. 3rd Movie Memory — 60
9. Bolt to the Future: Rehabilitation — 64
10. Dad's Notes: A few days in... — 70
11. Medically Speaking — 73
12. Shenanigans and Such — 79
13. Ins and Outs — 87
14. Christine's Visit — 97
15. They Told Me — 100
16. Rewards & Challenges — 107
17. 100 Days — 116

18.	Bolt to New Reality: Coming Home	117
19.	HOME	123
20.	Reality	127
21.	SIBLINGS	130
22.	Home ... According to Christine	136
23.	Bolt from the Past: All. Hell. Broke. Loose.	139
24.	Bolt to the Middle	141
25.	Reshaping the Bolt ... Moving Forward	145
26.	Living with the Bolt	149
27.	Beyond the Bolt	170
28.	The Ponytail	179
29.	Bolt Revisions ... Life Changes	184
30.	Epilogue	188
APPENDIX		197
31.	Gallery	199
32.	Crack!!!	204
About the Author		206

Chapter One

The World Went White!

Jonathan's Account

6:29 pm June 3, 2009

"Call them in," the umpire said.

Play stopped; sidelined. "A storm," he said

Clear blue skies and white billowy clouds hovered above us. Stopping play, foolish to an eleven-year-old. Sports were life. I lived to play, run, compete; my forte. My identity. Success found me on playing fields, tracks, and stadiums. I wanted to play, always, all the time. With teams, neighbors or siblings, give me a ball or a challenge. I rose to it!

My quick ambling feet were a gift, out distancing most peers. I played to win. Thrived in trying. Many victories fueled my passion and expectations; "A Born Natural".

Telling us to "hold off", wait, seemed ridiculous, unnecessary. "Crazy!"

Cole and I were throwing buddies — his Dad the coach. Eager to play, we asked to go to the outfield and throw.

"We'll be fine," I said, like I knew.

We got some throws in, suddenly without warning...

THE WORLD WENT WHITE!

No sound, just the brightest white light appeared, covering everything. Blinding, stark, complete white consuming every part of me and the world I knew. Filling me! No sensation, no feeling, just WHITE.

***

THE DREAM-LIKE STATE WASN'T ON EARTH.

IT WASN'T HEAVEN EITHER.

Like the beginning of a movie, a big white screen filling my world. Like before the words or logos appear, the very beginning of the beginning, ***WHITE.***

The movie starts, *"She"* is beside me.

Frantic chaos filled me. We are in a city; the Apocalypse exploding. A bomb goes off, bright orange fires rage, buildings collapse, bedlam, consuming, scary.

A window opens downward, an aerial view: I see myself fall like a rag-doll to the ground. My parents sitting "Criss Cross applesauce" beside me. Out of nowhere, they come flying in a hovercraft with a glass dome like aliens. "Don't worry Jonathan, everything is going to be all right," Mom says.

"What is happening? Why?"

A large city with a dark backdrop under attack. Everything on fire. Crumbling. Falling apart. "Who? Why?" Unsafe. Overwhelming Confusion. Shock. Panic.

"She" seems familiar, safe. "She" is with me.

I trust her, only glimpsing the hem of her dress and feet. We move, run, search safety, maneuver the craziness imploding. Seeking survival in this bombed out, massive-flaming city filled with pandemonium. Nothing makes sense; my life is threatened. *This is no casual movie.* I am the main character and it/something/someone is trying to destroy me. I feel the darkness looming in the distance. It is personal.

I AM THE TARGET!

Looking through a funnel, I watch myself lie on the earth. I am small, diminished by distance. The fires and noises of the collapsing city behind me. I am very aware it is all still happening, but I sense peace when I look down in the craziness around me. After Mom spoke, everything backed up, got smaller; the city faded in the background.

As the movie ended, *"She"* was no longer at my side. I saw her kneeling beside my body on earth: *"The Lady"* in a red dress and red shoes, Ferrari Red. Her face never revealed, but her essence felt ... safety, protection. She was reassuring, an angel to me, but perhaps not in reality. This place did not register as heaven.

The movie ends, panning farther and farther out, higher and higher, earth, the peep hole, smaller and smaller; I lay on the field, Mom, Dad and *"The Lady in Red"* kneeling, watching over me.

My body is there, but I am here at a vantage point miles above. *"The Lady"* did not speak, yet communicated much. This dimension is foreign, yet as real as life to me.

I was thrust into it by the WHITE.

***

Beyond the Story

There are many parallels to Jonathan's post strike account and what was happening physically in his body.

A possible correlation occurs between what Jonathan was experiencing in 3D, an Apocalypse, and what was actually happening inside his body. The lightning started fires in his body, traveling from his head down through his torso, down both legs, exiting between two toes on each foot. Every part of his body was touched, making him a torched inferno inside, like an electrical fire following wires and pathways through a structure. His organs taking hits like fuse boxes exploding. Physical networks collapsing and fire consuming a city. Literally, producing char, burns, and broken down systems.

It seems sensible that his brain was processing the physical reality into another dimension.

The thunder came well after the strike of lightning. The bomb in the 3D city was, likely, the thunder on earth. His sister explained… the sound came after the blinding flash and "sounded like several bombs exploding in synchrony!"

His movie world recedes, representing his heart stopping and organs shutting down.

It makes sense to say Jonathan was living in the spiritual realm what his body was experiencing in the physical.

"The Lady in Red", however, cannot be explained in the physical. Jonathan believes she was his guardian angel, sent to protect him through the journey. She is the first but not the only one who gave him guidance and protection through his journey beyond … **there are more**!

Chapter Two

Mary Washington Hospital

Judy's (Mom) Recollections

Jonathan was in cardiac arrest for approximately 43 minutes.

He died on the baseball field and remained dead for 43 minutes before a pulse returned.

I arrived at Mary Washington Hospital after Mark (Dad) because I dropped our other two children, Christine and Jeromy, at a nearby church.

"Are you Mrs. Colson?" the ER doctor asked.

"Yes."

"We got a pulse on Jonathan." He led me to Mark.

After what seemed like hours, the medical staff said we could see Jonathan. I did not know what the actual situation was. I thought we'd go back, hug Jonathan, all three would cry, they'd keep him overnight and we'd go home tomorrow.

Reality was far removed from my expectations: More shock set in.

Jonathan was intubated; breathing by machine; hooked up to many devices. He was unconscious and didn't even know we were there. It was surreal, heartbreaking, devastating.

It became apparent, this was an unpredictable journey. I quickly erased expectations from my internal white-board. Ecstatic, my son is alive, but no idea what that means or will mean. We may never again hug or cry together. His blue eyes may never light my day. To hear him say my name aloud was a far stretch. To sit by a baseball field or athletic endeavor looked like "not ever gonna happen again." Hopes and dreams obliterated.

He was ALIVE!

We'll start there and, prayerfully, not go backward.

"We'd like to Medi-Vac Jonathan to Richmond. Because of the storms, we will have to transport by rescue squad." I rode in the front seat, talking to my boy through the interior window. Heavy rains and lightning surrounded us as we traveled. Every part of this whole situation breathed intense, oppressive, foreboding, weighty.

Life hung in the balance, my son's life!

"Jonathan, You're going to be okay. Mommy is here," I repeated over and over on the hour trip. Squad members were on radios talking to Medical College of VA Hospital (VCU). Mile markers, exit numbers, status updates given constantly.

It would be a long time before we could hug or cry together. And a very long time before he came home!

I left assuming Cole's injuries were not as serious because he stayed at Mary Washington Hospital. I prayed for him and his family, happy for them. Over 24 hours later, Mark told me, Cole passed! More shock and unbelief. It never occurred to me. I was sickened. Numbing grief invaded me: tears, sorrow, unrestrained mourning poured out of me; I was blindsided.

***

Mark's (Dad) Memories

"I thought Jonathan had been struck in his belt area and thigh, down his leg. That's where I saw burn marks at the field."

Walking into the Emergency Room, the squad attendant told me, "We got a pulse."

I was out in the large waiting area with other people and a lot of commotion. Eventually, they separated us from Cole's family. We were still confused.

"Matthews family." The attendant said, ushering them back into the ER to see Cole. We pitched on the edge of our seats waiting for those words; they didn't come. Instead, we were escorted to a private waiting room. We assumed Jonathan was dead.

Later.

Maria, a nurse from an adjacent ball field who saw the strike, ran over to help. She came to Jonathan first and began administering CPR. She followed to the hospital and gave us updates.

"He's alive!" Maria exclaimed.

"We had no idea! I could read the shock and severity of the situation on her face and demeanor. This was our first miracle, but a teetering one with little promise."

"He is going to be transported to Richmond, MCV. Due to the weather, it will be a ground transfer," she informed us.

"Would you like to ride with him?" Judy was asked. She was whisked away to the ambulance.

I went home to gather necessities and Father Riley's phone number, then onto Richmond.

Chapter Three

Before The Bolt ... Childhood & Elementary Years

Born with a twin sister, Christine, life has been "extra"!

Activity was a constant: "outside" my playground. I loved animals. All animals: cats, dogs, turtles, frogs, birds, etc. My favorite stuffed Elephant hung out in my bed every night. Exploring trails and the creek behind our house, was my daily pastime.

My sister says I was curious, hyper, impetuous and had no boundaries! "He was annoying, couldn't chill out."

Dad built a swing set with a treehouse and monkey bars: good call. An energy consumer, I needed it.

Oh yes, and sports. Always sports. Any sport. Balls. Any balls. All balls: kickball, dodgeball, soccer ball, baseball, etc. You name it!

I ran "like the wind." Lacing up shoes, moving feet and covering distance felt natural, easy and fast! Always fast!! Real fast!! Winning races were my legacy. I knew early on I was "light on my feet" and "born to run"! My feet followed my wishes, taking me wherever I desired. When I willed them to speed up, they did! I didn't think about it. Written in my DNA, I never questioned: it was me.

Watching Barney, playing with action figures and farm animals, Care Bears, Littlest Pet Shop, Super Mario, visiting relatives in PA, sucking my thumb, prayers every night with Mom bent over my bed, a special blanket and my elephant capture my memories of early childhood.

***

Mark (Dad)

"Jonathan was a ridiculous athlete. Played quarterback, left-handed and right-handed … ambidextrous. Even as a baby, he could balance himself remarkably!! His nickname in Football was 'the hit man'! He was an intimidating tackler! His body was fast, but his heart was caring. I remember him saying, 'I don't want to hurt anyone.' His physical ability amazing to watch! He would jump, climb, walk across things. He slid down steps on his belly laughing and giggling as a young babe. It was incredible watching him among his peers. A gifted athlete; born that way. Every coach's dream pick."

***

Kindergarten:

There was Pam!

From day one, we were together. School was a win; I had "one more day to talk to Pam." She became my daily spotlight. I asked her to be my girlfriend, and she said "yes". Life was good!

I recall free-hand drawing Lilo and Stitch creatures for her after each episode. I drew a lot in elementary school … not so much since the accident. "You've got to tell Jonathan to slow down with these pictures, my refrigerator is full." Pam's mom told mine.

We used the new jungle gym at recess. Pam and I played that game where you throw balls into a bucket with four holes.

Physical Education was my fav. No surprise there; physical activity my passion.

***

First Grade:

Pam and I were in the same class again. I did everything with her!

Supposedly, somewhere during Kindergarten, we got ***MARRIED***! I wish I had a clear memory of that!! We were inseparable.

***

Christine (Twin-sister)

Pam and Jonathan got married in Kindergarten, at recess. Jonathan must have asked Pam to marry him and she said "Yes". Dad told Jonathan, "If you find a girl you want to marry, just ask her." Jonathan's always been impatient!

Jonathan doesn't remember, but I do. Girls don't forget these things. At least Pam and I remember. In fact, Pam commented to me in High School, "I guess I'm still married to Jonathan, we never got a divorce."

***

Baseball entered my life this year; becoming my world.

Christine and I played on the same team, the Pirates: instant love. From 1st grade till my accident ... it was baseball, baseball, baseball ... it was everything to me. (Baseball and Pam) Trying to improve became an obsession.

Christine was better at bat than me at the beginning. I worked to remedy her batting prowess; the last game of the season — I got a hit! I was running to second base. I went facedown; having never slid into base. My helmet and mouth filled with dirt. We celebrated and stopped for ice cream on the way home. When we got home, a message on the answering machine informed us; my Dad's Mom passed away. Indelible moments one never forgets. Lots of my grade school memories revolve around what did or didn't happen in baseball.

Sadly, this was the last schoolroom Pam and I shared till 11th grade! Arguably, the best two years of my life!! We hung out at recess. We saw each other outside school: living close to each other. Our families became friends.

***

Second Grade:

I remember a huge kickball feud. Our class divided into two teams and we'd play each other; the Wildcats and Bulldogs. It was quite a rivalry. Big Time serious in Second Grade! Schoolmates were fussing, crying and arguing about which team they were on. Everybody wanted to be on the winning team. All the whining and tears was "kindergarten stuff" to me. We were second graders. I volunteered to switch teams to stop all the "kindergarten behavior". Boys acting like that made me mad. Turns out, my friend Devin and I were the only athletic kids on my team. Even now, I describe myself as a "lightning bolt" around those bases.

It's ironic, "lightning bolts" and a ball game. That analogy described me even then; in my own mind!

Writing appealed to me. Ms. Joes would give us a writing-prompt for free writing time. I suppose with my drawing, I enjoyed creating: dreaming up stories and putting them on paper appealed to me back then.

About this time, I recall our punishment at home being a wooden spoon. I recall thinking my Dad was proud of me. When punishment needed to be given, Dad would come into my room, put the spoon on my bed and he'd put his hand on my butt and clap it with his other hand. It was me and my Dad's little secret. I would cry and scream. My Mom didn't know. My dad had a soft spot for me. Everybody knows now. Christine now says, "and ... you never got your spankings!" She's right.

We played recorders in second grade. I didn't learn the recorder AT ALL! During the culmination concert, where all of us were to show off our gained musical skills ... I moved my fingers but never blew one breath into the recorder. You can't accuse me of being dumb just because I didn't have musical abilities. I'd draw all kinds of unwanted attention to myself if I played. So, I self-preserved. Bravo to me!

This year, my baseball team was the Orioles. Both of my parents attended the games. When I started playing with my left hand, I realized I was ambidextrous. I later learned my legs are too. Both feet kick with equal strength. Baseball got all of my attention: I had no other hobbies.

***

Third Grade:

My baseball team was the Astros. That's about all I remember!

***

Fourth Grade:

My friend Cody gave me a new video game for my birthday, Animal Crossings. I was trying to learn the game: he gave me a book about how to play. I read it every chance I got. One day during silent reading, my teacher saw me reading the game book and told me it was "not acceptable reading material". I kept the book in my desk, switching it out when I thought she wasn't looking. One day, she caught me reading the game book again, so I switched it real quick and held up the other book when she asked. I felt so guilty. Tearfully, I made my confession: I lied. Lesson learned, I never did that again. She forgave me and didn't punish me.

My White Sox team won the Championship!!!

I usually pitched, but this year, we had two good pitchers on the team (myself being one), so I agreed to catch. There was a learning curve: I liked it. Catchers get to request time out for a water break. Cool. Feeling a sense of power, I tried it out. Not meaning to I picked a strategic moment in the game. Several of the other team's players were on the base. Their coach didn't hear the time out call, so he sent his players around the bases. The ref called back the runs communicating I asked for a time out. They were steaming mad! I truly did not strategically plan it; just wanted to see if I could stop the game! I did!

I practiced batting, all the time, in the batting cage Dad built at home. I was now one of the best batters on the team. Dad also put a pitching target in the cage, so I practiced pitching bucket after bucket of balls.

***

Fifth Grade:

Christine and I were finally in the same class. School changed a lot; we rotated to four different teachers.

I suppose Pam was my first girlfriend, but this year, I count as my first crush, complete with all the emotions of a pre-teen. Rachel and I were friends. We knew we liked each other. I knew two other large football type guys liked her too. All year we were friends. Rachel told me the other guys didn't like me and said bad things about me.

Those two guys were athletic, one of them, John. When we picked teams for kickball, he would be one team leader and I the other. It seemed if he kicked a home run, I'd kick a grand slam. I didn't mean to "one up him" — it happened, anyway. He probably took it as a competition, but I didn't mean it that way. When it came to sports, I tried my best.

Near the end of the year, about a week before my accident, I found out it was John's birthday. In art class, we had free art, so I made him a birthday card — I didn't like people being upset with me. "Everyone was my friend" is the lens I lived through. After I gave him the card, he was nice to me.

All my friends knew I liked Rachel, and she liked me ... all year. June 3rd, my friend said to me, "Why don't you ask Rachel out?"

"What does that mean?"

He explained, "It means you're boyfriend and girlfriend."

"That's it. That's what I'll do!" I thought, if that's what guys do, that's what I'll do. So, as soon as possible, that day, I asked her. I guess I shocked her; she didn't know what this "going out" meant either. "I'll think about it," she said.

At the end of the day, I was a hall monitor. She passed me on the way to the bus. We looked at each other, but she said nothing. She didn't give me an answer.

That evening.... my world changed forever....

Several years later, Christine told me when she went back to school, post-strike and cleaned out my desk, she found a note inside from Rachel. It said, "Yes!" She threw it away thinking, it wasn't important.

While in the hospital, I thought about Rachel, but did not think of her as my girlfriend. Just my friend. I never knew there was a "Yes!"

I hadn't thought about Pam for several years, because I didn't have classes with her and spent little time together. I remember when I was coming home, several people were on the sidewalk at home: Cody, Christine, her best friend, and Pam. My eyesight wasn't good and so I saw someone with long, dark hair. I asked my Dad, "Is that Rachel?"

"No, that's your friend Pam," he replied.

***

Rest of Rachel's Story:

I went back to school in January. I had little to no feelings — like a child, emotionally. Frustration was identifiable, liking things or having preferences was clear, but preteen emotions didn't seem present. I lived with simplistic emotions, like a child. My insides still seemed unconscious...

Valentine's Day came around and our school was selling love beads you could give to people. Rachel bought and gave me love beads ... I looked at them in my hands and felt speechless. I felt no emotions and didn't know what to do or say. She walked away. I seriously felt nothing and certainly didn't know how to respond.

Later, I found out someone, being immature and cruel, told her: "Jonathan loves you." I don't know if that spurred her on or if, while I was away, she thought of us as boyfriend and girlfriend. Maybe she thought I got the note. I'm not sure. I wonder.

***

Fifth Grade Continued:

I went back to pitching for the Yankees this season.

I recall driving to the game on June 3rd; Mom, Christine, and my brother were in the car. Mom gave me instructions about when we got there because we were running late. Nothing seemed unusual this week or night. I had no premonitions.

The game got delayed because of thunderstorms in the distance. It was sunny on the field, but the Ref wouldn't let us continue the game. I was talking with my friends on the sidelines. I asked my coach's son if he wanted to throw. His Dad warned us about the thunderstorms. I vividly recall saying, "We'll be all right."

I'm told we were standing between 2nd and 3rd base throwing.

One minute throwing a ball; the next everything went WHITE.

No sensations, feelings, or thinking, just WHITE!

No other words fit, only... **WHITE!!!**

Chapter Four

White FLASH! Blinded!

Family Accounts

***Christine (Sister)* ...**
FLASH! BOOM!

"**What the heck?** I went blind! What is going on? No precursor ... stark pure light from blue skies. Everything around me eclipsed by white. Out of nowhere, WHITE, blinding white!" "Barely regaining my sight, the BOOM sounded like a bevy of grenades in one harmonious blast. A boatload of synchronized land mines ignited. My ears popped .... deafening!"

Instantaneous!! No Warning!!!

As my eyes and body adjusted, I saw my twin brother, Jonathan, falling from the sky in left field, like a rag doll tossed in the air. His body crash landing 30 yards from where he stood prior. His teammate from center-field, Cole, in similar motion, now lay still next to him. Blue skies and clouds.

"WHAT just happened?"

Lifeless… Still! Running, screaming, crying, scattering, confusion, random, unexplainable… Pandemonium. Following the light and boom, the baseball field exploded into utter craziness. Fear seized me horribly. My racing brain tried to figure out this chaos. Blinking, pausing, no change. Wishing to erase minutes. Searching for answers … Wait, what? I should do something, anything.

"WHAT JUST HAPPENED?"

Glued to the bleachers, frozen in shock and terror, not knowing. Eleven years of experience held no context. Mom walking to the car, my older brother beside me. People took charge — carrying Jonathan off the field. Barking orders. Screaming, shouting, talking, not sure who was listening.

"What can I do? What should I do? Is this real?"

Moments before I was at my brother's baseball game. Where am I now? Bizarre, foreign, unrecognizable, senses reeling. Heart racing, grasping and gasping, sickened, clouded confusion. People were thrown backwards from this force cast upon their bodies, later hospitalized.

"Is this a dream? Can I wake up? Please, let me wake up! Let me go back to the baseball game!"

I was being pulled… a former coach, kept me on the bleachers: obstructing my view. Then, he scooped up my older brother and me, taking us to Mom's car. I asked him what happened; he said, "Your Mom wants you to wait in the car."

My brother said, "Lightning!"

The coach ignored it. "Your Mom wants you here. She's taking care of it."

"Lightning" … that's the first time I heard it.

"Is he right? Is that what just happened?"

"Oh my God, Dad, if you see a boy in a Yankees baseball jersey, please hold him, hold him while he's there, but please send him back. Please let him come back. Make sure you are with him while he's there … that's Jonathan…" Mom jumped in the car, these words spilling out of her mouth.

We never met our Poppa. Mom was, now, describing Jonathan to him. I'd never heard Mom talk to Poppa. If Mom thinks Jonathan is where Poppa is that means Jonathan is dead?!? Mom was trying to make sure Jonathan had family around him in heaven. What is going on? Everything random, our world invaded, turned into utter confusion.

We got left at a nearby church, supposedly with Mom's friend, Ms. Lavonne. Turns out, she wasn't there. Mom's boss also went to that church. Mom left, instructing someone to call Ms. Lavonne knowing she would come get us. Mom went on to the hospital.

Still not sure what the LIGHT or BOOM was!

We ended up at Mom's boss's house for the night. He and his wife were kind and caring, even though we didn't know them extremely well.

Nothing was explained.

It's serious, that much I knew.

***

Mom ...

"Delay of game," the umpire shouted, "Everyone off the field." Blue sky's with white clouds above. Distant dark storm clouds could barely be noted; no urgency. Adults surprised: boys antsy.

Returning chairs, halfway between the car and field, I heard Jonathan, "Don't worry Coach, we'll be all right." I noticed he and Cole walking back on the field. A sliver of intuition questioned him going back out. Walking back from the car, intending to get him off the field, the BOOM hit! Like a bomb detonating, fireworks exploding. I witnessed the look on the Coach's face as he ran onto the field. I ran to the fence. Noticing a distinct ozone smell, I saw two boys lying still, between left and center field... I ran out.

> ***One was Jonathan****: Face up, One leg bent oddly, Arms at his side, Left eye half open: something I will never forget. Shock, fear, dread, brokenness set in.*

A gentleman carried Jonathan outside the fence and laid him in the grass. Immediately, an ER nurse, Maria Hardegree, whose son was playing on an adjacent field, appeared and began CPR. I asked if I could help.

"Do you know CPR?"

"No, but tell me what to do." She did.

I knelt by his head after Maria's husband ran over and replaced my CPR assistance.

> "**Dear Heavenly Father,** I know you have your son Jonathan in heaven with you now, but I am not ready to let him go, so I am asking, please allow Mark and I to continue raising him. Please dear God, Please God, I can't go through life without him. In Jesus name."

Followed by "Our Father's" and "Hail Marys" over and over again. Pleading, Begging: ***I never prayed out loud before, ever!***

Noise, confusion, sobbing, commotion, etc. was loud. The pelting rain began drenching and chilling us. People kept wanting to move Jonathan into a car and Maria kept taking control and saying, **"NO!"**

The emptiest, sickest feeling filled me. It would be weeks before this surreal dream world... shock... would start to fade.

His right eye open and left eye half closed. The top part of his cleats blown off, missing, gone. His socks, still on, charred and melted to his feet. Baseball cap was still in place with a hole where the lightening entered his body.

"Mother radar" at heightened alert, I noted where Christine, Jeromy, and Mark were. I assumed Mark was praying too!

The rescue squad arrived. Bringing over a gurney, *"Bring the board,"* Maria insisted firmly. (a hard surface making CPR more effective). Only then did she allow squad members to take over.

I called Father Riley from some man's truck, "Jonathan is dead, we need you," I left the message.

"Intubate," I overheard from squad members. I knew he wasn't responsive or breathing. "Mark, we gotta go!"

Functioning outside myself, I hugged Cole's Mom in the parking lot, bound by the worst kind of catastrophe, forever.

"You follow the ambulance," I told Mark. "I'll take Christine and Jeromy to Spotswood Baptist, I'm sure Lavonne is there!" It was Wednesday evening — I knew she'd be there.

She wasn't. I looked everywhere and had people looking everywhere. Urgent to get them secured, I spoke with someone who knew her. They insisted they would get the kids to her. I agreed.

The sun was now shining! I hustled for the hospital.

As I drove myself to Mary Washington Hospital, I was having a conversation with my dad who passed away 20 years earlier. I said, *"Dad, I know you are a Big Pittsburgh Pirates fan and you are meeting your grandson, Jonathan for the first time, the boy in the Yankees jersey. I need you to stop hugging him because I asked God to spare him and allow him to come back to us."*

This conversation calmed me while I drove because my dad could always make me feel better, no matter what I was going through. I wasn't sure what to expect when I arrived at the hospital, but I also knew, when I left the field, Jonathan was with God and was not in pain. I kept praying for a miracle and for my dad to send Jonathan back.

The worst dread, in all the world, filled me...

"I may never see his eyes again."

***

"Are you Mrs. Colson?" the Doctor asked as I entered the ER.

"Yes."

"Well, he's got a heartbeat," he said.

"Thank You Jesus," I thought, the worst was over!

I saw Cole's parents in the ER; I remember seeing them holding each other. Then they separated us.

Cole was not being transferred, so I assumed he had fewer injuries than Jonathan. 24 hours passed before Mark told me that Cole passed. I felt physically sick, shocked and disbelief. I faintly remember a pastor coming to the ER from Spotswood Baptist and saying, "I am going to go see the other family, now. They need me more." I didn't get it! It never occurred to me!

Thoughts, experiences, meanings, life was in disjointed pieces ... nothing fit together!!

***

Dad ...

Four minutes ago, I left the ball field for home. The game delayed, I was hurrying home to prevent further storm damage to our driveway. The storm last night left it eroding; more rain could cause bigger issues.

I told Jonathan I was leaving and why. He said, "Ok, Dad, I'll see you at home."

I left the parking lot. I hadn't gone three miles ...

My cell phone rang. "Dad, Jonathan's been struck!"

Arriving, I saw Jonathan in a grassy area off the field. CPR being administered. I prayed.

I'll never forget the ozone smell in the air. We are told people's arm hairs were standing on end like supercharged static electricity, even head hair. People from adjoining fields confirmed the smell and the supercharged static electricity.

I knelt at Jonathan's feet next to Judy. Everything was in slow motion, like a movie ... a dream world ... an alternate reality!

"I instantly thought, I would never talk to him again... he was gone... the way his eyes looked. Even though it was a bright sunny day, his pupils were tiny, fixed and unresponsive. His clothes removed ... colorless, white, pale, purplish body. No shivers of cold, even though he was soaked. His eyes opened, never moved."

Maria's husband, kept saying, "Maria, look at his eyes! Look at his eyes!" She looked but never stopped CPR.

I thought I'd never see him alive again.

Surrounded by noise, chaos, and confusion, two victims, we started praying out loud "Our Father...". People joined us in the prayer out loud, maybe six or ten people. A Chorus of prayers. I don't know who they were.

The medics brought the padded gurney; Maria said forcefully, "We can't put him on that. Bring the backboard!" They returned with the board. After several attempts, he was intubated and oxygen started.

I left my truck in the parking lot, windows down, soaking the interior.

As the gurney wheeled through the ER doors, I heard,

"We have a pulse!"

The large waiting room was a bustle of confusion and people. They called Cole's family back to see him. We immediately thought, he was alive and Jonathan dead — our explanation for not being called.

After a bit, they separated us into a private waiting area. Eventually, Maria, who was in the room with Jonathan, came to update us …

"He is alive!" We didn't know! "He is alive!"

Looking back, we had no idea what that meant. Not seeing him till many hours later, in Richmond …no clue.

Maria informed us, "They want to Heli-Lift Jonathan to Richmond, but storms are preventing it. He and Judy will travel by ambulance." (An hour away)

Judy's boss drove me home to gather necessities and to find a way to reach Father Riley. I found a number for a woman, I thought, might be able to reach him. I called it. "I am standing in line for confession, and Father Riley is hearing confessions right now." I explained it was a life and death situation. She handed her phone to him. He closed confession and left to meet us in Richmond.

Judy's boss and his son, in separate cars, drove me to Richmond.

***

BEYOND THE STORY

Bolt from the blue: A positive lightning bolt which originates within the updraft of the storm, typically 2/3rds of the way up, travels horizontally for many miles, then strikes the ground.

Bolt from the Blue:

A *bolt from the blue* (sometimes called 'anvil lightning' or 'anvil-to-ground' lightning) is a name given to a cloud-to-ground lightning discharge that strikes far away from its parent thunderstorm. A 'bolt from the blue' typically originates in the highest regions of a cumulonimbus cloud, traveling horizontally a good distance away from the thunderstorm before making a vertical descent to earth. Due to the final strike point being a significant distance from the storm (sometimes up to ten miles away), these lightning events can occur at locations with clear 'blue' skies overhead - hence the name.

While many 'bolts from the blue' are **positive flashes**, some are not.

You estimate the storm to be at least 15 miles away. It sounds like a serene scene, right? You're safe. Or so you think.

Suddenly, an arc of electricity launches out of the top of the storm, propelling upward and outward at 20,000 mph. The mega lightning bolt shoots horizontally from the storm cloud; it targets a field just 100 yards away, and suddenly a flash brighter than the sun illuminates the landscape like day and blinds you. Your hair stands on end, your teeth chatter, and your ears are deafened as the thunderous roar shakes your house and rattles the window panes. A second later, it's over — yet every electrical device in your home emits a cicada-like hiss as the electrical field propagates outward from the blast. A foot-deep hole, three yards across, marks the spot where the lightning struck.

Chapter Five

Bolt from the Night

A Boy with Dreams

"Dreams have been part of me for a long time."

"Dream" Jonathan's Journal: 3-5-14

I've been having some really weird dreams lately. Are these dreams trying to tell me something? I don't really get what's going on. But it has to mean something. It has to! Doesn't it? They're all about the same thing; this is really weird. I wish I knew what it meant. Like Joseph told the Pharaoh what his dreams meant.

My most vivid dream was a "God Dream".

Just an ordinary night, long before the accident in 3rd grade, with lifelong impact. Spiritual impact. It began my personal journey with God.

I think I told Mom about it, but she might not even remember. I don't make a huge deal of things. This dream changed my life, before and after the accident. It has undeniably has shaped my personal relationship with God.

Brought up Catholic, I went to CCD Classes. Went to church every Sunday. I knew things about God, but didn't really understand what they were talking about. It didn't all make sense or fit together; church, God, life. Christianity was facts, sayings, rules, prayers, stories, sacraments, attendance, etc. Real life seemed separate from these practices and information.

I said evening prayers. I repeated words/prayers I was taught to help me learn to pray. I knew prayers, but didn't know God. I knew about Him. I respected that these were the ways to God and the way to interact with Him.

I **hated** going to church. I didn't get it. I didn't say too much because I knew church was expected and my parents thought it was important, but the importance was lost on me. Somehow church, my attendance and pew-participation meant something, but I was a kid who liked sports, competing ... sitting still was not my forte. Church was a long drawn-out hour of stuff that didn't seem to interplay with everyday life. In my heart, I hated it.

Till this night: My Turning Point!

I call it a dream, because it occurred during my sleeping hours. It was quite vivid and real — life-changing real ...

> *The Virgin Mary stood in my dream surrounded by Angels. Not as a statue, but as a real live person. The angels real and alive too.*

I woke shaken. Something very real just happened to me! God pulled back a curtain and authenticated all I'd been taught. It filled me. It's not a story, not something to just learn. Not words from a Priest. Not information. Mary is **real**. God is **real**. The Bible is **real**. A huge connection bridged in my 8-year-old mind … It's all true! It gripped me. God showed me His truth in a very graphic way. I've never doubted since that night.

I woke saying out loud, "I love going to church!" I immediately wanted to respond in a big way: "Mom, I want to be an altar boy." The only way I could think of to serve God. I wanted to serve Him, know Him, honor Him … He was real and now, personal! I had to respond by giving back.

I knew I had lots to learn, but wanted to serve.

I began Altar Boy training. It's the first time I think I tried to understand who God was. I always thought something about going to church made God love me. After the dream, I knew God loved me and I **had** to love Him back.

Serving as an Altar boy taught me a lot about the mechanics of Mass. Every time I carried the cross, I was nervous. I was doing something that symbolized matters of faith to the attenders. I was helping everyone experience God. I assisted the Priests in the traditions of faith which all held spiritual meaning.

Our Priest, Father Riley, became a very instrumental spiritual figure. He taught the Altar Boys behind the scenes. I watched his devotion and commitment to God. He held some outings for the Altar Boys' families. I recall going on hikes — at the top of the mountain we stopped for Bible readings, then prayed together. We were encouraged to contemplate God while looking at His creations, praising God.

***

"Father Riley"Journal: 3-17-14

> Father Riley is so awesome. He is a true man of God. He is always there for you plus he's wise. So, I can always go to him for advice. We are close, largely, because he walked with me through my journey. He gives me great advice when I don't know what to do. I guess I'm just clueless. I don't know many things. But if I've learned anything from being with Father Riley, it's that you don't worry about the future. You focus on this point in your life. If you don't know what to do, look to God for answers. God answers your prayers in different ways. God gives you an instruction booklet about what to do in life and that's the Bible! I hope to be as wise as Father Riley when I grow up!

I perceived Father Riley as a humble man. Caring deeply for the families in his parish. He preferred God gets credit, not himself. He was approachable, kind, always available. He had a large impact on my faith. He became a family friend. To this day, He keeps in contact with my family.

I was an altar boy till I graduated High School, missing some time after the accident.

In middle school, I started reading the Bible on my own.

I developed my personal way of praying each evening. Before the rosary, I say, "I am dedicating this rosary to...", then kiss the cross. I then go around the rosary, when I get back to the cross, I look at it, hold it up in front of me, like I am looking face to face with Jesus. I talk to Jesus for about 10 minutes about whatever is in my heart.

Through every year of my life, my faith has grown. I do not take my faith lightly. I feel I've been given special dreams connecting me to God. I am extremely blessed to feel it so personally.

***

"Easter" Journal: 4-5-15

> Jesus Christ is risen today, Hallelujah! Easter is a day dedicated to the Lord. Even if some people try to make it something different. Easter excites me for eternal life in heaven. I will never forget that Jesus is the one true reason for Easter. I was honored to serve today next to my brothers, the Bouchard boys. I cannot thank God enough for the many gifts he has given me. However, I deserve none of it. I am a sinner. But, I have still found life with the Lord. Sometimes I disappoint him, absolutely. But, I always try to repel Satan and his evilness. It's definitely not easy. Satan will try anything to bring you down. He's a lowly snake. And sometimes, I fall to him. I renewed my promise with the Lord today, that I rebuke Satan and his acts.

***

I wish everyone could experience the same monumental event to lead them to God. I can't explain why it happened to me or even it's full meaning. But, what I do know is that it was REAL. In every sense of the word, that morning getting out of bed as a young boy, I was different. I can't unsee it, forget it, or deny it.

It was a lightening strike of another origin; a spiritual one. A bolt from the night. It blew up what I knew, coursed through my body. Set my spiritual world on fire. Rearranged my preconceived thoughts — gave physical life to spiritual concepts. Shed light on areas of little understanding. Burned a living image into my heart. Authenticated God. Changed me forever.

However you wish to describe it — vision, mirage, or dream. (I contemplate it's definition.) My relationship with God and faith are forever molded by it's appearance to me!

I Am ... a Boy with Dreams... and Faith.

Perhaps, this spiritual "Bolt from the Night", was preparing me for the future "Bolt from the Blue."

***

"Priorities" Journal Entry: 6-29-14

No matter how much other people mean to me, I have to keep God as my number one priority. He does so much for us and most people don't give him any time. One thing I never really get is why does he keep doing it. The terrible things that humans do. I just wonder how he can still love us and never give up on us. I feel sometimes I get caught up in video games but in all reality they mean nothing. Sometimes, reality is more important than games. When I die. I can either go to heaven or hell. That's reality. I need to start shaping into the godly figure I can be. I can't go down that path! It leads to eternity in hell.

***

"Apocalypse" Entry: 7-14-14

The Bible describes the apocalypse as the time God will put an end to the earth. He tells us that he is the Alpha and Omega — the beginning and the end. This is also called Judgment Day — when God decides what after-life people deserve either to spend eternity in heaven or gruesome eternity in hell. God already told us for sure he will never again wipe out the earth, like the flood. He'll destroy the earth he created in different ways. Whether in volcanoes, earthquakes or by sending the death Angel here, as he did in the time of Moses.

Only God knows when Judgment Day is coming, but it's sooner than we think. I know not to ever underestimate God.

Chapter Six

Medical College of Virginia (MCV)

Hospital #2

"Once we get him in a room, you will be allowed to see him."

We arrived before midnight. We waited hours. They were assessing, running tests … making life and death decisions.

Father Riley arrived, around one am. He was allowed to go to Jonathan … last rites were given.

We were all in the waiting room when the doctor came in…

"The lightening struck Jonathan on the left backside of his skull, went through his body and exited between both of his big toes."

Two exit wounds were surprising. Lightning normally enters and exits from one location. The doctor asked if they could take pictures of his head, his left leg where the lightening arched out at his shin, leaving him with third degree burns on both his head and left leg.

Being a training trauma hospital, they'd never seen injuries this severe. The Doctor explained, "Jonathan will help teach doctors for the future, if the situation presents itself again."

Father Riley left, assuring us he'd return.

***

The CHAPEL – 2 am

"I really feel like I am being called to the chapel," I told Mark. "Will you go with me?"

"Yes."

We knelt at a kneeler at the front. We prayed silently. "Please allow Jonathan to live and stay with us. I don't care in what capacity. No matter what, I will take care of him! Just let him live," I kept repeating.

At the baseball field, I prayed, "Let him come back" ... he was gone then. Passed away.

Here I prayed, "Let him live!"

As I prayed, what I can only define as the Holy Spirit, sent a sensation starting at the top of my head and progressed all the way down to my toes; like chills or shivers. I knew when they ceased, I was done.

I turned to Mark, **"He's going to be okay."** I just knew, I felt it as I was praying. In what capacity, I didn't know! **"Jonathan is going to live."**

I felt like I was done there. I had been obedient. I visited God and He visited me.

We returned to the waiting area.

After he was stabilized and run through countless tests, about 4 am, we finally got to see Jonathan; in a PICU cubicle.

***

Pediatric Intensive Care Unit

"He has about a 4% chance of surviving by the markers we see. Let's see what happens. It's a waiting game."

> "We have a treatment that hasn't been used on brain patients, but we would like to try it with Jonathan. A cooling bed. It might be the only thing we can do to help him. It will lower his body temperature, really low… experimental. We'll give him something not to shiver."

> "When there is damage or an insult to the brain, the neurons which give communication in your brain, start to bang together and sever each other. That is when memory loss occurs; it cuts off the circuitry. We think we can help that by

forcing the brain to think everything is normal ... keeping his temp from rising. Hopefully, saving his brain function."

We agreed.

The Doctor told us Jonathan's strike was on the top left part of his head. The lightning arced out his left shin area and exited between both his big toes.

That explained why the tops of both of his cleats were completely missing ... blown off.

Overall, he looked normal. His color had returned — from ashen grey at the field, to pale pasty. His head was shaved and a tube had been inserted into his skull to measure intracranial pressure.

For over a week, I sat by his side in a recliner. I could not leave him. I sat on the edge of the unknown — prospects were iffy most days. We could fall off the cliff at any moment. Or, be asked to climb the mountain back to health and a new normal. Either way, I was not leaving his side. Facing Jonathan's and our future one-moment, machine-beep, breath-at-a-time.

Whatever the outcome, I wanted to live it with Jonathan, every moment of each unfolding day.

***

Critical Condition

He was in an induced coma and on a cooling bed to cool and maintain a lower body temperature.

He had two big circular bars, both filled, lines everywhere. Things were pumped out and in. In some of the "out bags", we noted charred material, signifying the extent of burns to Jonathan's interior.

He was set ablaze on the inside by the lightning. Like a building being struck by lightening, it burns outside and inside. I pictured electrical wires in a house catching fire, progressing through walls and into other rooms. Similarly, his internal electrical wiring was burnt from head to toes and every organ in between taking hits like circuit breakers and fuses, popping, hissing, igniting. It was sickening, heartbreaking and life-changing. Threatening Jonathan's life.

They weren't sure how long to leave him on the cooling bed, so after 24 hours, they started to warm him back up. His pressure started rising, so they cooled him down again.

Mark left at night to get a few hours' sleep at the Ronald McDonald house.

After about a week, Mark said, "We've got to get out of this room!" Food was unappetizing. Hunger didn't occur to us. We had sick stomachs all the time. We snacked from a basket our neighbor, Beth Yorio, brought.

Mark began bringing food to me. Slowly, Mark convinced me to leave the room for a bit. We'd walk a block or two and come right back to Jonathan.

I sat in the recliner praying the rosary like a chain smoker on cigarettes. As soon as I finished one, I'd start another. I covered myself with a prayer shawl Beth brought for Jonathan. I put it on him for a short time, but I wasn't allowed to leave it. So, it felt right and comfortable to wrap in it. Sometimes, it felt like a cocoon we were morphing inside of. Sometimes, a large wrap holding my life together. Oftentimes, it's warmth calmed me, soothed me, shut out the world and helped me focus on my communication with God. It was also a covering, reminding me many people were praying for us.

When I wasn't praying, I talked to Jonathan. They told me to. "Mommy loves you Jonathan. You were in an accident. Don't be scared. There are lots of people praying for you. You are going to be okay." "Jonathan, this is temporary. Be strong and when you need strength, pray to God and He will comfort you."

They told me my words would connect with his subconscious and make him calmer, part of Holistic Health. I later asked Jonathan, "Do you remember hearing me talk to you?"

He said, "No!" I sort of chuckle, now. I did all that talking, talked myself to death! He doesn't remember. Hopefully, it meant something at the time. Maybe, it just kept me occupied.

I kept up with work on my laptop, if they had a question. I got some texts on my phone, but Mark was the one giving updates. The majority of the time I said rosaries, shifting my gaze back and forth between machines and Jonathan.

Eventually, I got comfortable taking a small break, during the day, leaving to sleep for a few hours at the Ronald McDonald house. During those times, Mark kept vigil. Every night, I couldn't leave. I couldn't do it. I attempted to sleep in the recliner while buzzers, alarms, talking continued, as it does in a Pediatric Intensive Care Unit. I could not find resolve to break my nightshift observance.

Leaving my eleven-year-old baby boy in a hospital bed fighting for his life at night was impossible. It was a "we" fight and not solo work for Jonathan to figure out. Mark and I felt committed and involved in his recovery, as if we ourselves, had been the ones lying in the bed. You could not pry us apart, convince us or reason us away. Our sole focus was Jonathan. Being physically next to him, was where my heart and body needed to be, however long the night.

***

Sad Night

One night, I recall being woken by alarms. I couldn't figure out what the buzzers were — the nursing station was empty. A young toddler girl, in a crib, had been admitted that day. I later pieced together that she expired that night. They were all attending to her. It sickened me.

We were well aware we were not the only ones struggling with a child whose life was in danger. We heard helicopters. Saw cubicles with other people, noticed comings and goings. We could not find comfort in knowing we weren't the only ones. It was a tragedy for all of us. But, it did bolster some faith to realize, we weren't the only ones experiencing this intensity of trauma with our child. Everything is not well and perfect in the world. We are standing with others in fighting for our son's life.

An unspoken camaraderie I cannot explain.

***

Jonathan's Team

Every morning we met with Jonathan's team. We'd hear a run down about the night, what they were looking at. I knew it was serious; didn't realize all the turns it could have taken. His status was up and down. I stopped trying to assess things. I'll never understand all they talked about.

The optimism that began with a "pulse restored", and continued with a "chilling" prayer time in the Chapel stayed with me. Later, a Doctor said he didn't expect Jonathan to live 6 - 10 days! "I'm glad he didn't tell us that," I told Mark!

Since then, I've learned that is the critical period for lightning victims. The medical community has to wait and see if the electrical disruption and "hits" his body took, prove permanent or if his organs will recover and regenerate. We had no idea... We thought he just needed some treatment, assistance and time.

"We are eternally thankful, that no one told us. All of the team seemed positive to us. We would have had a much different experience had we known their expert expectations."

***

Critical Moments

Jonathan developed pneumonia, presumably from aspiration during CPR. It caused fevers and took more than one antibiotic round to clear up.

Days In. ... "Let's see where this kid is at," the doctors agreed. (I never liked the term "kid".) "We'll start backing him out of the medically induced coma, and see how he responds."

Seeing his accurate condition, unmasked by sedatives was a critical assessment tool.

"When he is waking up, he should start getting restless, especially pulling at his tubes," they told us, which would be positive. If he started contracting to a fetal position, that would be a concerning sign.

I waited and watched like a hawk eyeing its prey. He never moved! Not a twitch of muscle, not a fluttering eyelid, nothing! Our hearts were sinking ... again.

While watching ... his numbers started elevating. They ordered a CAT Scan of his brain. His cerebellum had stroked. There was swelling in his cerebellum — causing fluid backup and retention, hydrocephalus. An emergency shunt was inserted in his brain, right there, in his PICU room. Another emergency situation, challenging Jonathan's life.

The shunt would drain the fluid, keeping it from going down his spinal column. They explained, "It would be a whole different set of issues to deal with." "This is not optional." We knew the tone. Every time his numbers hit a certain level, they drained it. The frequency kept escalating.

They put him back into a coma. All his numbers kept rising. Another CAT Scan ... his brain continued to swell ... blocking the drains. The only option was to put him in surgery and remove a section of his skull, to give his brain ample room to swell and heal... Posterior Fossa Decompression.

I was debating whether or not to allow the surgery. I had a feeling we could lose him! They adamantly said, "You *need* to sign it!" I did.

This all escalated quickly from weaning off meds, distress, shunt, fluid worse, to surgery! We were scared and helpless.

Life and death hung in the balance so many times. Every bit of hope dashed with a number or test result. Watching your child lie still and lifeless was torture enough. Giving up control and decision making — helpless and unnerving. We were the ones entrusted to care for him, yet, in this situation, we were ill-equipped to know how or what was best for Jonathan.

As much as our hearts ached to see him healed, we were deficient in knowing how to accomplish it in these critical situations. We prayed endlessly and trusted our medical team. It was all we could do and the best we could do. It was foreign to our years of parenting. The hardest of days. Shrouded in the prospects of death with pulses of hope captured and collected like fireflies in the darkest night.

When death loomed closer, we held up our "firefly torch" in the dark castle. Taking the next step and waiting for a strand of light to enlighten the next. At times, our little jar held only one luminescent fly .. the hope of intervention by our Master Physician. He was with us. We knew. We felt. His presence was enough and, often, all we had.

When life stepped forward, we celebrated like cheering throngs brought to their feet by a grand slam.

The roller coaster ride you take when life and death swirl around is dizzying. Gripping the security bar with all the strength one can summon. Pits in stomachs with unexpected drops. Smashing corners. Knocks, double vision, squeals, sighs, muffled hearing, exhausted emotions.

"Please, someone make it stop and return us to the platform where everything and everyone is well and stable, once again!"

We held on with all our might and relied on God with our whole heart!

***

Jonathan's Journal: 9-1-15

Everyone needs to know God was a major key to my family getting through my accident. We couldn't have done it without Him.

***

After the Surgery

After removing a portion of Jonathan's skull, things progressed positively.

Three days later, they started to wean his medication and bring him out of the sleep coma again. This time nothing escalated.

Six days after surgery ... **He woke up.**

***

June 14th

"He tried to push us away," the ecstatic nurse shouted.

First Voluntary Movement! Major Milestone!!

Later that night, I said "Jonathan, can you open your eyes for Mommy?" His eyebrows went way up on his forehead. Moving his eyelids looked as strenuous as lifting weights!!! Finally, he DID IT, his eyes opened. Not very far or for long, but his baby blues were showing! His beautiful blue eyes opened; an eternal two weeks since those eyes looked at me!

Unforgettable! Ecstatic! Part of him was back.

He was starting to look like "our Jonathan." His face and feet were not as swollen. Progress was happening.

He stared, daze-like. We weren't at all sure anything was registering. He didn't communicate.

The Doctors kept waiting for a sign. Something that told us his brain was functioning. They warned us it would take days for the medication to leave his body.

***

The Sign

"Get the nurse. Get the nurse. She needs to see this," Mark screamed.

About three days after we saw his eyes, around noon, the sign appeared. Mark was talking to Jonathan, holding his hand. They had a secret handshake for years, made up of seven different moves. Mark started the handshake with Jonathan, and he slowly responded accordingly. He showed no glimpse of communicating with his eyes, but his hands were responding appropriately to Mark's stimuli.

Because Jonathan was not breathing, dead, for 43 minutes, they were very concerned about his brain function. Was he oxygenated enough to support brain health? They thought, the strike could have caused the wiring to short circuit, frying his neural connections.

"I can't take any credit for this! This is higher than me!" the Doctor exclaimed.

We were ecstatic, screaming, bursting with relief, joy, and thanksgiving ... so relieved and happy. We saw a sign of the Jonathan we knew. If he could remember "the handshake" after everything he's been through, it would only take time for the rest. Mark was so happy and relieved, an altogether different person.

Tidbits at a time, we were all making our way back to a new normal. This was a milestone reached, a corner turned. Praise God.

A monumental day!

This is what the Doctors had been waiting for ... a signal of cognitive function!! His brain was working!!! He communicated through his hands.

Everyone was exuberant, celebrating ... the room could not contain the excitement. I am sure other rooms heard lots of noises. Hugging, jumping, clapping, rejoicing ... it was the moment we all realized, he truly was alive again!

43 minutes of death, now swallowed up in life!

We didn't know, yet, the end game, but we were abundantly hopeful!

Jonathan was dead. He is, now, ALIVE!!! ... more than just a heartbeat, he has brain function!!!

MEDICAL COLLEGE OF VIRGINIA (MCV)

Thank you, God ... uncontainable joy and thanksgiving!!!

Lots of phone calls and updates were sent out that day!! It was every bit as life changing as the Lightening Strike itself. Hope was restored and life revived.

As one rehab Doctor put it,

"Jonathan, you are Lazarus — Walking!"

Lazarus was not resurrected in perfect human form. Lazarus stank when Jesus called him out of the tomb. He had wrappings to be unbound before he could walk and live the way he did before his death. John 11:38-44

Jonathan's restored heartbeat was the first sign of his rebirth. Jesus calling him forth, if you like. The visit from the Holy Spirit in the chapel was a confirmation of things to come, the hope of life being restored.

Today, *this day, when cognitive function could be measured, was the day his healing body started limping out of the tomb!!*

There were still many steps to take, much rehabilitation, grave clothes to be shed.

This moment, we watched him rise from a lifeless sick bed and begin his climb to the mountain summit — restored health! Glory be to God!

Every step a victory! Small victories large, large victories .... miracles!

Jonathan wasn't fully awake and not always responsive. It takes days for all the medications to clear the body, until then, we wouldn't fully know. The last three days he was in MCV, he could have been moved out of PICU. The team decided to keep him and discharge him from the PICU because he would have had to share a room with another patient.

We were able to push him around in a wheelchair. One of us would push and the other would hold his head up as he wasn't able to. He didn't assist in any way. He had no facial expression or reaction to his surroundings, even on our short walks.

We were thankful he was alive and made it through the strike. If that was how he was going to be forever, we'd take care of him. We had hope: the Medical Team didn't think he'd live this long, now, rehab was approaching.

Twenty Two days after entering, June 25, 2009, we left the Pediatric Intensive Care Unit at the Medical College of VA. Jonathan was transferred to Kluge Children's Rehabilitation Center in Charlottesville, VA, part of the University of Virginia Health System. The real work began.

Jonathan left with profound hearing loss on the left side, Nasal Gastric Tube for feeding, burn wounds on scalp and lower extremities, and an IV port for antibiotics.

He does not remember any of his stay in Richmond except the dreams mentioned in other chapters. He has returned many times to see Doctors, Nurses, and participate in medical conventions. They remember him and he, now, knows them. He is well aware of the life-giving role they played in his life. The care he received by this team, saved his life.

The cooling blanket may have been experimental for preserving mental capacities, but it certainly worked for Jonathan. Their foresight and willingness to try any and everything they knew about, afforded Jonathan an amazing recovery... smashing his four percent odds of survival with no percentages of regaining ordinary life functions.

Miraculous!!!

***

Beyond the Bolt: Therapeutic Hypothermia (Cooling Blanket)

In 2010, American Heart Association strengthened its position based on a growing body of research. Because therapeutic hypothermia is the only intervention shown to improve neurologic outcome, AHA now advises clinicians to consider therapeutic hypothermia for any patient who can't follow verbal commands after return of spontaneous circulation. It also recommends transporting cardiac-arrest patients to a facility that can provide therapeutic hypothermia along with coronary reperfusion, advanced neurologic monitoring, and standardized goal-directed care.

What was experimental for Jonathan, has now become the recommended standard for treatment!

Chapter Seven

2nd Movie Memory

I HAVE NO CONCEPT of time between the lightning strike and waking up at Rehab.

I cannot put this scene into context. It could have been while I was dead or while I was in a coma. ***I do know ... it is real and realistic!*** It's a memory to me, not just a dream. I am convinced it happened and played a vital role in me being alive.

After the first movie scene closed with me lying on the ground and the "The Lady in Red" ... kneeling with my parents beside me, this is my next memory...

> I was an infant in a hospital; a light peaceful place. Happy. Soothing. A nurse was taking care of me while Sponge Bob played on repeat on the TV.

> This nurse was my constant companion. She had a light in her, pure light. I seemed attached to her. Our hearts were joined, in sync. We were always together. We went on little adventures throughout the hospital. I was at the crawling

stage of development — she let me explore. She was fun and entertaining. I felt safe, loved, cared for.

One day, we were together: I crawled onto a mail conveyor belt. The kind that packages move along to be sorted. I remember it as happy until... a dark mail shoot appeared at the end of the belt. I could see packages drop off into blackness. Fear gripped me. I tried frantically to crawl backward to escape the shoot and inevitable lostness in the dark. As hard as I tried, I was losing the battle; the end of the belt kept inching closer.

I couldn't keep up; black and darkness loomed. The happy serene setting became threatening, ominous, inescapable, suspenseful.

I started falling, feeling doomed, no return, and blackness. I thought it was the end.

At the very last possible second, my nurse grabbed my foot and pulled me back into the light. She saved me!

Her face was unseen, but her ponytail was epic. It was beautiful to me. It rang familiar and comforting. Brown, long, simple curls and sways, the way it was tied and hung. Memorable, crazy, but I'll never forget it. Imprinted on my memory, it is synonymous with being alive.

She saved me! The memory of her still does save me. For my life, it will always be a symbol of being saved out of darkness.

After being saved, we returned to my room and continued watching Sponge Bob.

At this point, I started seeing things through my nurse's eyes. She was outside of the room looking into my room, far off. Maybe from the nurse's station or a window into my room. I saw Father Riley give me a Teddy Bear while I lay in the hospital bed. Watching myself from outside the room: I took the Bear and hugged it tight for a while.

When I woke up in rehab, I found out Father Riley did give me a Teddy Bear while I was in a coma. He laid it in my bed. In reality, I never interacted with it. I was incapable. Yet, in my spirit state, watching myself, I did hold and hug it. There was an unseen dimension to those watching me lie in PICU in that hospital bed. I struggle to explain it to someone who has not experienced it. It sounds unreal. To me, it was real and it happened.

I still have the Teddy Bear.

***

If that part of the story can be validated as true, why wouldn't the rest be true, as well? I certainly believe it's true. It's one of my experiences, as real as playing baseball or arguing with my sister.

Perhaps, it coincides with my moment of death or a time at MCV when my brain was swelling, and my numbers were rising. I'll never know exactly. I do know the Teddy Bear is real.

I later found out the ponytail was too!

Chapter Eight

3rd Movie Memory

This movie memory happened sometime before I woke from unconsciousness. I have no reference for when exactly it occurred or if it occurred directly after the other two. Scenes seemed to open and close. The only sense of time I had was day and nighttime inside of the memory.

***

I was looking through my own eyes but felt like an infant.

We were at my Uncle Mike and Aunt Chris's house in Pennsylvania: we visited every year for vacation. I knew it was their house, but it didn't look exactly like their house. It was a "heavenly" type house. I felt comfortable, familiar, like the many times I visited.

My cousins Paul and Anthony were swimming, having a great time in a huge glassed indoor pool. I was watching the fun. I had no sense that I could or should join them. Like I said, feeling like an infant, or maybe, my inability to do anything made me small or unable to join my cousins. I was a definite observer: not communicating with them in anyway.

Later in our visit, I was sitting with my Mom, Uncle, and cousins in front of a TV ... watching a Sponge Bob 2 movie. (There never was a Sponge Bob 2 movie made.)

At nighttime, my mother slept by me.

Sometime during this visit, I went alone downstairs to the basement. It was dark but had enough light to see. I don't recall walking or crawling, I just moved to the basement. Like a non-human mode of transportation.

Sitting in the basement, was my Poppa, my mother's father. I never met him — he died before I was born. Immediately, I recognized him from his war picture in our home. In this place, I knew him like any other person in my life. I didn't act surprised to see him or communicate with him. He was not a ghost or presence. He appeared like a flesh and blood person. I was not frightened to see him. It felt like a natural relationship, not someone I never knew. There were no introductions or physical touching.

"Poppa can I stay down here with you?"

"No," he said, "you have to go take care of your Momma. You can't stay here." "Go back upstairs," he said **speaking with wisdom and authority.**

There was no choice! I knew I had to follow his instructions. I left Poppa and transported to my mother.

***

In this memory, I met a grandfather I've never known and inquired where I belonged. For some reason, I must have wanted to stay with him. "Why" is not clear to me. But I did ask to stay!

He guided me back to my family, upstairs ... I translate that as .... sending me back to human life. I could not stay where he was, beyond life!

When I woke at Rehab, I didn't have to try to remember these memories. They were real; implanted in my mind and heart. No one had to ask or prompt them to the surface of my memory. These memories vividly surfaced like any other memory I lived through; part of me.

Learning much later, from Christine, that my Mom was talking to Poppa in the car leaving the ball field, has made this memory all the more captivating.

> "Oh my God, Dad, if you see a boy in a Yankees baseball jersey, please hold him, hold him while he's there, but please, send him back. Please let him come back. Make sure you are with him while he's there ... that's Jonathan...", my mother said in the car after the strike, passionately and emphatically.

I did see Poppa! I asked him if I should stay with him!
My Poppa did as Mom asked, he sent me back to her.

***

All sorts of questions emerge...

Did an angel take the image of Poppa for instruction and familiarity? Was I between heaven and hell? I never sensed it was heaven or hell, even though, it didn't appear like earth. Maybe, it was a "waiting room"? Did the "coma" that surrounded me make vivid dreams seem real? Why did my memories/dreams make sense with other pieces in real life, if they weren't real?

How did my mother's instinctual prayers guide me and give me instruction when I was clinically dead? My Mom's words to her deceased father were not in my bodily presence, so I couldn't have heard them in my physical ears. I was in an ambulance on the way to the hospital. She was in her car driving my brother and sister to a friend. She instructed her Dad, Poppa, to find me, send me back ... and ... **HE DID**!

It's ironic, my Mom saw me on earth in my baseball jersey, lifeless, with no heartbeat ... dead. Yet, she prayed to Poppa, in the afterlife, to look for me in my baseball jersey. She knew it was physically on earth, she just saw it. But, somehow thought it would translate to my afterlife.

Perhaps, when staring at death, eternity is apparent. Without even realizing it, our minds traverse between the two. What we know in our present reality, seems possible and real in the beyond.

I have no grand explanation or understanding of how this all happened. But with my whole heart, I know it did. I experienced it. It is a piece of my journey beyond life. I feel blessed and fortunate to say it returned with me and is now part of this, my present life.

Ecclesiastes 3:11 ... God has set eternity in our hearts.

Chapter Nine

Bolt to the Future: Rehabilitation

"Same Old" Jonathan's Journal: 9-26-14

When you grow faith in God you finally grow faith in yourself. And that's how winning gets done. That is key to winning every type of game you can think of. Why do you lean on God and let him help you out? He said, "I'll carry you through anything and everything."

***

June 25th: Jonathan Moved to Kluge Children's Rehabilitation Hospital in Charlottesville, VA

My eyes were open. I'm told I had a hand sign for "Yes"and "No". Mom says, I didn't smile. Just stared into space and slept a lot. I don't remember any of it. I don't remember Mary Washington Hospital, MCV or being transferred to Rehab at Kluge.

I'm told for the first few weeks, I was in a wheelchair, one person pushed the chair and one held my head up. I didn't have the strength to hold my head: severe muscle loss, weakness and no tendon strength. I wasn't responding to things around me, just staring. No facial expression.

As my meds were decreased, I slowly came back to life. My brain remapped, finding new ways to function since my cerebellum was severely impaired. The lightning strike zapped it good, leaving me with lots of deficits. The experts explained that my brain would attempt new pathways to make my body function. How well those pathways successfully healed and rerouted would determine my abilities.

As my brain awoke, I remember feeling paralyzed. I couldn't even move my head. I felt trapped in my body-shell. I'm told I wasn't paralyzed; my brain just couldn't connect enough to move my limbs and muscles. Also, muscle atrophy and tendon strength contributed to lack of movement. I sure felt paralyzed! I couldn't figure out what happened!

I was plagued with double vision for a while but couldn't tell anyone! To an extent, I figured some things out, but could tell no one. Eventually, I was treated for the double vision.

What I couldn't figure out was ...

HOW DID I GET LIKE THIS?

How did I physically decline so traumatically? In my mind, it was like nothing ever happened. I was talking to myself wondering and responding. This didn't make sense. My brain woke up remembering the Jonathan who loved athletics and was the fastest runner, always. I was also the boy who could and did talk to anyone. They say I had "charisma", a person people were drawn to: engaging, kind, with lots of energy.

Where did he disappear to?

Who am I?

I felt like a baby. I couldn't communicate, speak. I couldn't move anything. I wore a diaper. I didn't even eat; I had a feeding tube. I felt frustration and anxiety. I got mad; pushed things and people away. I was not a crier as a kid. I tried not to cry! Personal injury did not make me cry. Funny, I used to protect my face when I was falling. (I referred to it as my "money maker!") Now, my natural response is to protect my head; hands covering my skull.

I don't recall physical pain when waking, although I was still on meds. I'm told, perhaps, the meds caused some of my emotional symptoms. They dissipated over time.

I thought I was pathetic. Look at me? How had I become this? I wasn't a baby by age, I knew that, but I was certainly baby-like in just about every way. I was totally dependent on others to exist. My dad would pick me up from the bed to transfer me to the wheelchair, like lifting a baby from a crib. I was helpless.

Why was I like this?

My brain couldn't fit the pieces together.

What was wrong with me?

Letters and written words made sense to me. I knew what they said and what they were. I retained that portion of my memory!

The doctors warned my parents I could wake up with total memory loss. Not know who anyone was or anything about my past. Including anything I was ever taught — letters, words, and speech!

Thank God that was not the case! I slowly woke up knowing everyone, remembering letters, counting, words, reading, etc. I just lacked the physical ability to communicate that I remembered! It was very frustrating!

When my hands started moving a little, they held a letter board down on the bed, so I didn't have to lift my weight saturated arms. All my body parts felt heavy, really heavy. I lifted one finger to point to letters, spelling words to communicate. It was long and arduous. Just a few words wore me out. I definitely wasn't communicating all I was thinking. It was too exhausting.

At one point, I signaled my mother the "I love you" in Sign Language. After a few times, she asked my brother what I was trying to tell her ... she had no idea. He said, "It means Rock On!"

From that point on, when she was leaving, I'd give the "I love you" sign. (I don't remember learning the sign, but it showed up in my actions, prompted by my memory, I suppose.)

She'd reply, "Rock On, Jonathan!" Every. Time.

I'd think, "What is she talking about?? Rock On??" I knew she was misinterpreting what I was trying to tell her, but I didn't have the energy to explain it. She thought we were communicating and I knew we weren't!

Weeks later, when my speech had progressed a bit, a friend, Ms. Beth, came to visit. I didn't speak fluidly. I tried so hard to speak. It took a boatload of effort, yet it sounded garbled and distorted. It sounded like how I've heard deaf people speak. I knew what I meant, so I overlooked how it sounded. I told her how I used this hand signal and how Mom made a confusing response, Every. Single.Time.

Later, Ms. Beth told my Mom, "He's saying, 'I love you.'" And you are responding, 'Rock On!'" Everyone cracked up. It wasn't the first or last miscommunication that plagued my recovery.

The day after my arrival at Kluge… we went to work. I was not there to rest, that was immediately apparent. I had five regular therapies to attend every day, consuming six -eight hours. Therapists: Physical, Recreational, Occupational, Speech, Academic. I had a small rest at lunch. Monday through Saturday. Sunday was a rest day.

***

June 26th: Day #1 of Rehab, Physical Therapy….

Crying and trembling, I stood for the first time in 23 days!!! It was painful, but I did it! A sense of who I once was washed over me. I wanted "ME" back. I was willing to do anything suggested to find the former Jonathan again.

I threw magnetic darts at a target, after the therapist massaged my shoulders to get weeks of kinks loosened. "He was obviously in a great deal of pain. But, he stood there like a champ and hurled those darts. We knew he had fortitude, but watching it in action, under such distressing circumstances was quite inspirational," Dad remembers.

My Schedule

8:30 am - PT

9 am - OT

9:30 - speech

10 am - School

10:30 am Speech

Break/lunch

1pm - PT

2pm - OT

As my strength built, the classes were lengthened.

***

June 27th: Day #2

The therapist asked if I wanted to try to stand up again. Without hesitation, I chose to try. I was motivated to gain what I had somehow lost. Dad says, "Watching was hard. I'm not sure I would have tried again the next day, when it was so difficult and taxing the day before. Jonathan, on the other hand, pushed himself at every turn."

Chapter Ten

Dad's Notes: A few days in...

***I was talking with Dr. Norwood** asking questions about Jonathan's recovery. He looked at me with a sincere look, like I wasn't being given all of the information.*

"Mr. Colson, come to my office." He sat me down and asked, "What are your expectations for your son's recovery?"

I answered, "We are going to go home and Jonathan is going to live a normal life."

He looked me and said, "Do you know the severity of your sons injuries?"

I responded, "I know he is going to go home and ..."

He interrupted me, "Have you seen the MRI's of Jonathan's brain? I need to show you."

"I think I have," I said, "but I don't know what I'm looking at."

He started showing me Jonathan's MRI and said, "This is like a raisin, this is not supposed to look like this," pointing to his cerebellum. "A normal cerebellum is the size of a walnut!" **"Can you see the difference?"**, he said, showing me a normal one.

"Yes."

"This controls speech, walking, balance, and coordination," he explained. "Jonathan's damage is considerable, like a major stroke; a lot of damage!" "this does not match your expectations."

"Well, we'll see," I replied.

"I want to prepare you for what you're going to deal with in reality," he matter-a-factly stated.

Dr. Norwood was trying to orient me to reality, but, I didn't accept it. I said with confident assurance, "No, he's gonna walk, talk, etc." To this day, Dr. Norwood remembers that conversation. His prognosis was far different than Jonathan's recuperation. I did not give up hope. I think that played a crucial role in Jonathan's recovery. We kept encouraging him and he didn't give up!

Don't ever be satisfied with a prognosis, fight with all you have. Jonathan was fighting. I was giving my all to assist him and so were his therapists and medical staff, family, friends, even strangers encouraging and praying for him. People need hope! We carried hope for Jonathan and eventually, he found hope for himself.

The human body is not altogether predictable. None of life is.

What are the chances of being struck by a bolt from the blue?

What are the odds of beating medical predictions?

Both can happen!!!!

Until you've exhausted every avenue, work hard and hold onto hope!

Even the experts in medicine will tell you it is not an exact science. The human body and spirit is amazingly resilient and can miraculously exceed all prognosis and expectations!

Dr. Norwood was trying to paint a realistic picture of Jonathan's future. We chose not to accept that picture despite the deficits in Jonathan's body.

We are so grateful that something in us — we believe God, spurred us on to hold hope and encourage Jonathan beyond his medical prognosis.

Dr. Norwood, with every good intention, thought I was in denial. He was trying to help me accept his reality for Jonathan. He felt the time had passed; I should begin accepting Jonathan's future. I, on the other hand, was optimistic. I wasn't changing my hopes in light of his education. I was convinced "life is what you make it." "A journey starts with a step." Judy and I were in total agreement. We were going to give Jonathan as much hope and encouragement as we possibly could to keep going and keep playing to win the game.

***

Years later, we were invited to a gala, at the Jefferson Hotel in Richmond, to bring awareness and recognition to people who provide care in pediatric ICU at VCU (MCV renamed) and to present achievements. Three cases were presented that night; Jonathan was one of them. Dr. Norwood and his wife were in attendance. We had a few moments to chat alone. He said, "You have changed my mind and thoughts. My training does not always know the outcome. There is the potential for another outcome; things can play out differently. Your outcome was not as I expected. I'll always be wondering, how you, Jonathan, did these things based on what I saw on your images and tests."

Chapter Eleven

Medically Speaking

The cerebellum does not heal or regenerate once damaged.

When you have a stroke, you damage the cerebellum. You only recover. Jonathan shouldn't have any balance at all.

He shouldn't have any hearing in his left ear. He has total detachment of his nerves to his ear drum. The doctors clearly stated that the part of his brain where he should be getting his hearing from is not functioning. His brain rerouted and the "mail is going to a different address. I don't understand how he's doing it," the doctor told us. His hearing is basically normal.

They expected Jonathan to have only "cerebellum speech": monotone. **He doesn't.**

They did not expect him to perform academically. They were preparing us and him to just be as self-sufficient as possible. They fully expected him to need care the rest of his life. Even teaching us how to do it. He was not expected to be totally independent.

***

June 29th: Day #4

Jonathan is settling in at Kluge. He's still throwing up several times a day. He's very tired and falling asleep in therapy. Therapy is six days a week.... 8am-3pm.

***

July 4th: Day #9

I Spoke My First Word!!!

Fireworks may not have gone off, but inside that rehab center, people's hearts, minds and tear ducts were exploding. A day very anticipated, hoped and longed for.... I answered a question by speaking a single colossal word.

That word was .... Poooorrrrttttttiiiiissss.

Barely recognizable, amid moans, groans and distortion, but spoken none the less. People talked to me all the time even though I didn't respond.

A Redskin (now Washington Commanders) diehard, I was outfitted in a team hoodie. "Who's your favorite player?" the Physical Therapist asked me. Everyone waited, as they had before ... Eventually, I got out the six letter word, "Portis"! Shocked faces, cheering, congratulations erupted.

My brain, finally, found a reconnection to my mouth!

At my afternoon Speech Therapy, Dad told the Therapist, "A lot has changed since this morning. Jonathan talked in PT."

"I don't believe it", she said. "No, he's speaking! Ask him who his favorite Redskin player is!", Dad repeated.

"OK then, Jonathan, who is your favorite Redskin player?" she asked.

I eventually, got it out one more time, "Poooooorrrrrttttttiiiiiisssss." She picked up a pile of paperwork, about six inches high, walked over and dumped them all in the trash can! Saying those six letters exhausted me like running a marathon. But, because I did, I didn't have all that work to do anymore! It was dramatic and extremely motivating.

Totally exhausted, I didn't speak another word that day. The amount of energy I exerted to say that word twice, drained me! Pre-strike Jonathan would never have imagined saying two words could be so physically and mentally difficult.

Rehab was foreign territory, but today was a .... new beginning! A triumphant day!

***

July 7th: Day #12

One month and three days since the Lightning Strike...

Christine and Jeromy (siblings) are both now home from Pennsylvania. Dad is living at Kluge with Me. Mom is back at work and comes down on the weekends.

***

Dad's Daily Notes:

Jonathan's still having problems with vomiting and diarrhea. It keeps him worn out. He's in school, at Kluge. He's now speaking in a very laborious broken way and is very emotional.

We chose to have one of us stay with Jonathan, always. Since Judy stayed at MCV 24/7, Kluge was my turn to take off work and help Jonathan. I stayed but most parents didn't, so it caused a different dynamic between patient/caregiver. It wasn't to make them feel like they should do more. They were doing a good job. I was going to be involved in my son's rehab, no option ... give me instruction and tell me what he needs and I'll follow through.

I administered all of his oral medication, the whole time. He did not want to take it! It tasted horrible and swallowing was difficult. Disguising it in pudding worked till he caught on. I had time to coerce and coax ... nurses didn't.

One day, Dr. Farenella, said to me, "Ya know, we really didn't know how to deal with you. We aren't used to parents who stay here with their kids. Some parents barely visit. You're on the other end of that spectrum. After a bit, we came to the conclusion you weren't going anywhere. About week three, we figured out ... you were here for the whole duration. At first, you were the topic of conversation. Then we realized, you weren't here to get in our way, but to help. You became an asset to us. It was a different dynamic for us to deal with. Right down to Jonathan's laundry."

It was a give and take relationship. I was respectful. I followed their plan, unless it was something I strongly believed wasn't to Jonathan's benefit. We had some talks.

***

Questions

"Why am I this way?," I asked Dad.

"You've been in an accident, and it hurt your head and legs. You are here to work on getting better," Dad replied. I was satisfied with that explanation.

The Doctors advised my parents to give me a simple explanation about why I was in the hospital. "Save the details for later." Waiting till I could communicate better, so I could ask questions and have a conversation was the route they took.

***

Swim Therapy

My parents chose Kluge predominately because of water therapy. They knew I would identify with it and thrive in it. They were right!

This pool was kept at body temperature all the time, 98.6 degrees. When tendons are tight, atrophied, not moved in months, physical therapy is done in the pool. Tendons become viable, they begin to move again.

I loved time in the pool. My body and mind felt "normal" there. I could do in the pool what I did pre-strike ... I was me. I could move!!! Being lowered into the water was a million weights lifted. My inept limbs and body reacted differently covered in water. No wheelchair, walking aides or assistance needed. Freedom coursed through my limbs. I felt glimmers of the Jonathan I was and could be again. I always came out of the water different. Inspired. Encouraged. Hopeful.

I wonder why every rehab doesn't have a pool. I am so very thankful it was available for me. My outcome would have been much different if the waters were withheld. In the pool, I found success. Other therapies were covered in defeat and immense struggle. Once a day, in the pool, my body could perform as I wished: spurring me on to try harder.

Chapter Twelve

Shenanigans and Such

Dad's Notes

"Bring my trunks, Judy."

"You're going to get in the pool?"

"Of course, I am getting in the pool. I don't care what I look like!"

"You're going to scare all those people."

The aquatic instructor knew if Jonathan was in the pool, Dad's getting in the pool! Wherever and however, I could help, I did. Maybe, I did scare them at first, but I was in the pool!

***

"You Were Warned"

I have had a unique habit as long as I can remember. I guess it started when I became independent at self-care.

In the course of my shower, I open my mouth and drink. Sometimes, I drink a lot, sometimes, not so much… depends how thirsty I am. I like the warm, hot water. It's part of my shower routine.

I was not allowed to drink water with the feeding tube.

My Dad warned the nurses, "You better watch him when you give him a shower, he will open his mouth and drink the water!"

I never felt satisfied or full with the feeding tube. I always felt hungry really. My mouth was often dry.

I suppose they didn't believe Dad or thought it was an odd or infrequent occurrence.

My first shower, Dad was present in the room, but the nurse was giving me the shower. I was in the hoist. The shower over head, out in front of me. When the moment presented itself, I did what I always do, opened my mouth trying to ingest the water.

I suppose the nurse was busy washing me and concentrating on what she was doing and wasn't looking at my face.

I took full advantage.

Dad blurt out, "Look! He's doing it right NOW!"

The nurse surprised, quickly responded, moving me away.

Dad was worried. They'd never handled my injuries before and felt overwhelmingly responsible about monitoring my care. They didn't want anything else to happen to me.

I imagine the nurse had never run into someone with my unique showering habits or skills. I wasn't going to pass up such an opportunity! The thought of warm water in my tummy made it irresistible.

They can't say they weren't warned.

***

Dad's Notes: Frustration

At this point, Jonathan was in the wheelchair only later in the day; as tiredness overtook him. He no longer needed it to shower. He was in the bathroom and I left, shortly, to grab towels. I started hearing loud noises, a ruckus, in the bathroom.... Jonathan was throwing things.

"Jonathan, What is wrong?" I asked.
"I want to know, how long I am going to be like this?"
"Jonathan, you can see your progress has been amazing."
"I know, but Dad, how long will I have to do things like this." "I've got stuff I want to do!!"
"With that attitude, son, you will do it!"

Coming back takes fortitude, perseverance, and loads of hard work.

Jonathan hated his wheelchair. I knew when he didn't fight being in the wheelchair, he needed rest. He didn't like the walker either, even when he really needed it! Moments of frustration came dramatically and unexpectedly.

***

I took my walker and flung it 10 feet down the hall...

"Jonathan, what. are. you. doing?!?," my therapist reacted.
I wasn't speaking well, but I tried to get it out... "I have stuff I need to do!"

"My God, you can't do that, you need it," he said grabbing my arm.

I got so tired of doing stuff... especially the walker. I didn't care if I could or not, I wanted to just walk right out of the hospital like nothing ever happened and nothing was wrong!

I couldn't wait for that day!

***

Shenanigans... For Good Reason

My bellybutton looked like a dartboard from the shots, every day. I despised those shots. My abdomen was so sore and the shots painful. I cried when the nurse appeared. They usually asked me to pull my shirt up. Doing so took every ounce of energy I could muster. I did not want to with all my might, but I succumbed.

To stop the shots, I had to walk 100 feet a day. The distance required to ensure my body wouldn't form blood clots from inactivity.

Dad promised me we wouldn't stay at rehab one day longer than necessary. I wanted to go home so bad. I learned early on I had to do my part to move closer to that goal.

I was motivated to stop those shots. As I was walking with my walker, I met a man named Mark who worked there . At this point, I had three "Marks"; my Dad, my physical therapist, and "Mark down the hall." I don't recall his title or what he did. But I'll never forget him! He provided motivation.

On his office door, he hung Cowboy headlines, being a fan. As a Redskin fan, they irritated me. So, we made an agreement — if I walked with my walker all the way to his door then I could tear off the headlines from his door!

Mark became my rival. My inspiration to walk and get rid of those painful shots forever. I'd gladly walk that hallway to rip off any news of the Dallas Cowboys, with glee. Then, I'd tape, where it hung, a clipping of the Redskins headlines.

Inspiration came from many places, unexpected and welcomed!

My rivalry carried over to the Physical Therapy room. One day, I went in and in front of me was a framed photo of Tony Romo, a Cowboy player, with **my** face taped over his. Written by the pic, *"Can you believe this traitor?"* Everyone had a good laugh.

I said, "No, No, I am being framed!!"

I took it down too!!!

Later, I replaced it with "Mark's" face taped onto Mark Cooley's face (a Redskin player).

Our rivalry went back and forth — a great distraction to my condition!

We learned later, that being on that shot was giving me more rehab time, per our insurance company. The Medical Team was not pushing my walking because they wanted to give me as much therapy as possible, even though the shots were painful. We didn't always fully understand all the reasoning, but we were certain everyone was working for my best interest. It took a large team of people to address my needs and help me function again!

"Mark down the hall" was a bright spot in many exhausting dread filled days.

***

Mom's Biggest Regret … In Her Words

Jonathan emerged slowly from his post-strike state. He came to Kluge with nasogastric tubes and feedings. Until his digestive system, chewing, swallowing, etc. was all back to normal, introducing food was a huge risk.

One weekend day, Mark and I were switching duties, likely so he could go sleep or shower. It was one of my first "solo" times with Jonathan. Jonathan was still anxious, not quite sure what was going on. On top of all the medical issues, he had become dependent on Mark being with him. I was not nearly as proficient at his routine and treatments.

I suppose having just me, gave Jonathan more anxiety than usual.

I promised him, "Mom will not leave you!"

Before Mark left, he wanted to speak to me and asked me to come into the hall. I tried to refuse knowing Jonathan was already anxious, but Mark was insistent I needed to hear something out of Jonathan's hearing range. I finally relented.

"I'm going just outside the door for a moment, Jonathan. I'll be right back!"

I returned in a few minutes to find Jonathan in tears. He had thrown-up everywhere: on himself, all over the bed, down to the floor … a huge mess and a very upset son!

My heart sank. I had betrayed my promise with disastrous results.

To this day, Jonathan reminds me, "You told me you wouldn't leave me!"

For many reasons, it stands out as a traumatic time to him and me. It broke and still breaks my heart.

I wish we could have handled those moments another way. We were all trying to survive this new world. The last thing I ever wanted to do was cause my son any ill feelings.

Yet, I did.

Sometimes, it's hardest to forgive yourself. I'd love to turn back time and choose differently in those moments.

It's now part of our story and we carry it with us. Time has lessened it's impact, but I know Jonathan and I will remember as long as we live.

I figure, there will always be regrets, but moving forward is most important and we have managed to do that, thank God.

***

FOOD

Ravioli .... OH YEAH!!!

It sent my taste buds reeling with delight. Extreme pleasure, glorious!! Old canned Mini-Ravioli, gourmet to me: my first food in months!!! Tube feedings kept me nourished, but I always felt hunger and a need to crunch and chew. Even soft food in my mouth was a huge step. To this day, I love Ravioli from a can! It holds a fond place in my memory, heart and stomach.

My first meal ... McDonald's Cheeseburger Happy Meal .... best food I've ever eaten!!!! I wanted so badly to chomp into a burger and when I did ... angels sang and the heavens opened.... glorious!!!

I am sure, shortly after, I threw up. I threw up a lot even after I was home. Zofran became my friend. Everyone was a bit uptight about my eating, scared even. Choking or aspiration were real concerns and could have meant grave set backs.

My dad was my food ally. After the tube came out, strict monitoring of "in and out" was required. The dietitian tried to get me to down horrible stuff. Dad often came to my defense, tabulating every morsel going in and weighing every ounce coming out. Many times, he proved my calorie intake was sufficient keeping me from having to ingest "the world's worst junk in a cup," a meal supplement shake.

He kept a private stash of food in the room; favorites. He made sure I'd eat by providing alternatives and options. You should have seen the Doctor's face when Dad opened the closet, which was stacked with food — my own food pantry.

"Where did you get all that," he asked.

"Kroger," Dad said.

"Go to the cafeteria and write down what you want and they"ll buy it for you," he said.

Dad never did, being self-sufficient as he is. He stashed applesauce (strawberry), Jello, pudding, Honey Nut Cheerios, Mac 'n Cheese, canned Ravioli, etc.

Dad enticed me with food. He hid medicine in chocolate pudding. Eventually, I caught on. I don't eat it anymore!

Chapter Thirteen

Ins and Outs

Bargaining

BLOODWORK NEEDED TO BE DONE AGAIN and I was very upset, tired of all the medical procedures and intrusions. Dad bargained with me, "Jonathan, you get through this, I'll get you a Twix bar out of the vending machine." (One of my favorites.)

"*Uh, he can't have that,*" the nurse said.

"*Yeah, he can have it,*" Dad said. "*You get through this Jonathan, we are going to sit out there on the patio and have a Twix bar.*"

The nurse looked at Dad like he had three heads, so he says.

I allowed her to proceed, she got her blood sample and Dad wheeled me out to the patio and cut tiny slivers of Twix bar, laid them on my tongue and I let it dissolve, sinking the flavor into my taste buds ... a fabulous treat!

Dad talked me into throwing most of it (3/4 he says) to a nearby squirrel. The squirrel picked it up like a lollipop and ate it while we watched. A wonderful distraction.

Thanks Dad!

Little by little, a sense of normalcy returned to my regimen. Slowly, I could do things I used to do. Eating was a huge step forward.

McDonald's became my Friday treat after a hard week of work.

Thanks Mickey D's for the inspiration. You gave a young boy the best meals of his life!

***

Dad's Notes:

Every day we saw small things improve. At the time, it seemed so slow, like we would never see a change or get to our desired goal. His sleep was very broken. Even in the middle of the night, I took opportunities to do things with him. Once, I saw a raccoon at the trash can out the window.

"I'm gonna get him up so he can see it. He loves animals."

I scooped him into the wheelchair and outside we went: watching a playful raccoon for a while.

A few nights, there was an albino skink who came onto the patio. We didn't venture outside, but I put Jonathan in the wheelchair and took him to the glass doors to see.

I looked for opportunities to break things up and distract us from the severity and difficulties we faced.

One sleepless night, I picked up a New Testament Jonathan was given and began reading. I believed in God and claimed Christianity as my faith. Something happened in that rehab room, as I read that testament. I found support, strength. It nourished my spirit. It became a practice for me. It was definitely my source of strength in the midst of all this craziness. It inspired me to inspire Jonathan.

So many people were praying for Jonathan and our family. I sensed that throughout our journey, but God's words written to me in the Bible was the spiritual food I needed to keep going. I can't quite explain it, but every ounce of me knows it was true!

***

Caregivers – Mom and Dad's Notes

#1 — We called her "Sunshine", after the nurse in the movie "The Story of Life." She was amazing, our favorite. She very expressively enjoyed her job. She was the best; very amiable and encouraging. She told us "keep talking to him, don't stop talking to him. Just like he can answer!" So, we did. She also taught Jonathan, thumbs up for "Yes", two fingers for "No".

#2 – Some people do their jobs and then there are people like Wing Ping. She was an angel. It was her calling! She had an over abundance of compassion for her patients. We will never forget her!

She was in the U.S.A. on a work visa. We can't recall which Asian country she was from. She told us of her house with a tin roof, dirt floor, very small. She rode the bus two hours each way to go to school so she could pass an aptitude test that got her into a program for nursing. Her goal was to come to the U.S.A. At the time, she couldn't speak English. If she couldn't pass that test, she was out of the program. She passed, went to the Netherlands and there got a visa to the US to work as a nurse. Her parents whole income was what she sent home from her pay every month. We remember her saying, "The existence of my family is on me. I send them $100 every month and they live very well there."

#3 — We had a gentleman tech who was an outstanding caregiver. He would start every shift with a joke. "Jonathan, ya know …," it started. He tried to put a smile on Jonathan's face, every shift. You just don't forget people like that.

#4 – A new face appeared one weekend. I think she was as Physician's Assistant. Maybe in her late 20's. She came dressed to the nines with lots of makeup. Jonathan and I both noticed the way she addressed his Physical Therapist, Mark. She talked more personally and was flirtatious with him.

We teased him! Little distractions like this kept things more normal and light. He sluffed off our teasing about her liking him and wanting his attention. Finally, we said, "We'll prove it to you. Next time she comes in, say, 'You have such natural beauty, I don't think you need any makeup!'"

To play along with Jonathan's (and my) game of distraction, Mark said those or similar words the next time she came in.

The very next day she arrived.... WITHOUT any makeup on!!

We all laughed for two weeks! It was a big joke between the three of us. Engaging caregivers passed the time; welcomed asides.

Mark teased Jonathan daily about the "girlfriend" he didn't have. Of course, he got responses from Jonathan. These were priceless gifts really. You deal with people everyday, it is the ones who try to make human connections we can't forget!

#5 – We have nothing but wonderful praise to give Jonathan's Medical Team at MWH, MCV and Kluge. Honestly, they were God sent, inspired, and designed.

At Kluge, we had weekly meetings with Jonathan's team. They were careful never to give us an end point or definitive prognosis. All their experience proved those things cannot be predicted or measured. They're inherently individual.

They instead noted his progress: what was being worked on, what would be worked on next. We asked lots of questions and got careful answers, respectfully.

We are so blessed they allowed us to participate closely in Jonathan's care and rehab. We realize it's not always this way. We believe it made all the difference to Jonathan's recovery.

***

Therapies

I hated Occupational therapy!

My fine motor coordination was NADA. Such aggravation: "Pick up these buttons and put them in the muffin tin." "Do this. Do that." Ugh, I got so frustrated! Getting my muscles and fingers to cooperate was the worst. She pushed me like a good therapist should, but it seemed I made the slowest progress ever.

Physical Therapy was a favorite. I made a deep connection with my therapist, Mark. I was an active kid, so activities in Physical Therapy appealed to me. Plus, I saw progress quickly.

I couldn't stand, I did stand. I couldn't take a step, I took a step. The noticeable advances motivated me. I moved from wheelchair to walker to sitting on a Yoga Ball playing Wii. Who doesn't want to keep going when such affirming changes are taking place!

I remember when I tried to walk, my Dad and Therapist would sing this song, "You put one foot in front of the other..." from the "Santa Claus is coming to Town Movie."

In Cognitive Therapy (School), the **Woodcock-Johnson** Tests of **Cognitive** Abilities was administered to me. "It **is** one of the most popular IQ tests. The **test is** used primarily to **measure** ability for academic achievement, oral language, scholastic aptitude, and overall **cognitive** skills."

Everyone with a brain injury is administered this test. They can tell how you will recover through your thought processes. It's a huge book. My teacher was responsible for taking me as far as I could go in that book; getting harder and harder as we went.

My teacher, with 30 years experience, did not let me give up. I would get so tired and weak, but she pressed us forward. She was getting ready to retire. She told me "I have given this test for 30 years. Never have I gotten this far in the book!"

I didn't think I knew information, but somehow my brain would call it forward and I would have correct answers when asked. I remember one Math test they gave me. I saw it and thought; "How on earth am I supposed to do this?" It looked so confusing to my eyes. It overwhelmed me wondering how I could finish it. In some inexplicable way, my brain gave answers to me. It happened in a moment: I started to do it! I was seriously shocked. "How do I know how to do this?"

After I went to PT, my therapist said, "I heard you did really well on your math test. That lightning strike must have supercharged your brain or something."

I never knew I was smart till that point. Information was obviously still in my brain. When I needed it, it showed up.

My brain was remapping and rewiring to skirt my deficiencies and find a way to trickle down into my mouth and fingers. The thinking section of my brain said, "Nope, I don't know that." The files in my brain said, "Hold on ... let me retrieve that file." And it did — to my shock and amazement!

Speech therapy was hard too — learning to talk properly again was a long arduous progress. Yet, the progress was easy to measure because it effected every part of my day. So, simple strides seemed instantly rewarding and encouraging.

When my twin sister first came to visit, my garbled speech sounded to her like an accent. Wondering how I got an accent from the lightning strike, she surmised the strike caused me to have a British accent. She didn't want to bring any attention to it, for fear it would hurt my feelings. Keeping her thoughts to herself, she thought her twin brother would just have an accent the rest of his life.

We laugh now! We were young, so much had changed... Why not a British accent too!!

It couldn't get any more bizarre than a Bolt from the Blue!

***

Outside

I felt like an elderly patient in a nursing home... being wheeled everywhere! It had been so long since I experienced "outside".

As a child, I played outdoors as long as I was allowed; jumping, climbing, running (always running), swinging, exploring, sports, playing tag, chasing friends and siblings, etc. It was my habitat; my home.

Months past since I recalled the experience of "outside". A distant faded memory, snatched from my daily routine.

I remember seeing the door. "I forgot there was an 'outside.'" I didn't remember how it felt. Hospital beds, medicine, treatments, and therapy rooms filled all my days. The "current" Jonathan was trapped in a foreign world of bed rails, wheelchairs, walls, rooms and medical teams. "Outside" was not spoken of or considered. It was my distant past. So far removed from my new reality, that it never occurred to me.

When they wheeled me out, my senses were immediately filled to the brim.

"WOW, the sky is so blue," I thought ... I wasn't speaking yet. *"Look at the green trees!!"*

The colors were so vivid and real. It made me so happy ... I had forgotten ... I'd been inside so long.

All I wanted to do was hop out of that wheelchair and explore. Seeing everything was stunningly new. Like getting freed from a cave!

At first, I felt a sense of freedom, then motivation. *I wasn't free yet, but I had a sense of it again,* it motivated me to fight for more. Work hard and gain every possible bit of freedom I could find.

Parts of me were coming back to life, even ones I had forgotten!

My parents continued taking me outside at every opportunity. Sometimes, I did recreational therapy outside too.

Filling my lungs with fresh air stimulated my body and will.

It was the sight and smell of freedom. Everyday I wanted freedom more. Freedom from medical teams, therapists, medicines, wheelchairs, physical limitations and bodily constraints. I wanted the freedom to be Jonathan again, not a patient, not needy, not confined. I wanted to run like the wind, joke with friends, eat whatever I decided, sleep at home ... be normal.

Being outdoors gave me hope, it could all one day be so; I would fight my way to being Jonathan again, one torturous inch at a time.

***

Communication & Visits

I had visitors at rehab, mostly on the weekends. Sunday was best: no therapies.

Father Riley visited.

After a bit, my siblings came. Eventually some neighbors and friends made the trip to Charlottesville.

We went to a lounge; played simple board games. I used two hands to pop the dice on the Trouble game. That's how weak I was. Remembering how to play was not a problem: the information popped to the front of my brain when I needed it.

I loved company. Even though, my speech was horrible and communication limited, seeing them made me feel normal and connected again.

Dad says, "Jonathan was never embarrassed! NO, he was happy, really happy. He wanted to catch up with his friends. I never, not even one time, saw him feel embarrassed or have self-pity, never. He was just so happy to be with his friends."

As I started to work with my fingers, I had this old flip phone. The ones where each key is three letters. I only remembered two peoples phone number: Faith Anderson and Jeffery Henafield. I decided to text them. I think all I ever texted was "Hey, how are you doing?" They answered but I was exhausted. I never answered or tried that again. It was too hard!

***

Dad's Notes:

It quickly became quite apparent to us, that keeping people updated could become a full time job. We needed to concentrate on Jonathan.

Our friend and neighbor, Beth, asked if we wanted her to be the primary point person to give updates to the community and friends. We were so thankful. Beth started a Facebook page and collected emails. Each day, we sent a text, email or called her and she took care of the rest. It was a godsend.

Our immediate family, we called. A very few really close friends — I texted. The rest went through Beth.

Chapter Fourteen

Christine's Visit

Entering his room, he looked helpless and small.

***"This sucks!"* I thought.**

I immediately crawled into bed with him. We were always next to each other. Proximity felt normal, being apart strange. I didn't ask to get on his bed. It was my natural reaction to being with him again. He didn't mind. We were together again, after our first separation ever. I guess when you share a womb, closeness is a given.

Jonathan was lying in bed with a diaper on; very skinny. In photos, I looked huge next to him.

He was so different. I knew everything was agonizingly difficult for him. I didn't know how to respond to all the changes. After a few visits, I adjusted and accepted his limitations. I mothered him, helped when I could, tried to comfort him.

He still says I "mother" him. I feel it my duty to protect him. It became part of my role as his twin sister, after the accident. Sometimes, now, he gets very mad at me for it, but it's natural. I don't really know I'm doing it till he calls me out.

At Rehab, I watched TV with Jonathan, all the time. The shows he chose were annoying to me; I put up with them. I felt so bad for him. Normally, I would not have been so congenial. I stick up for myself; especially with Jonathan. We're equals ... "sass" tumbles out of me when my mouth opens.

When I first heard Jonathan's voice, it sounded like he had a British accent. I listened carefully and he kept sounding like that, so I thought ... this is his voice now! We laugh about it now. I guess I wasn't either told how difficult speaking was for him, or wasn't listening when I was told. As an adult it sounds absurd, but as an eleven-year-old, that's how my mind translated the change in his voice. As a result of the strike, I, now, had a British speaking twin brother!

Mom and I went up to Kluge every Friday. During the week, I'd stay with her friend while she was at work since it was summer. I spent all week without Jonathan; I couldn't wait for Friday. I couldn't get enough of him. Seeing him was my favorite part of each week. I didn't care anything about his injuries, deficits, or differences. I wanted to be with him.

I was always sad when we left on Sunday; the worst part of my week.

I recall one weekend visit in particular. It became medically necessary to transfer Jonathan to a hospital. Immediately I cried, thinking he was getting worse again, scared. They put an oxygen mask on him. Jonathan saw me visibly upset and he put up the "ok" sign with his hand to comfort me as they wheeled him away. It did!

***

Back to the Hospital

A few weeks at Kluge my blood pressure dropped dramatically. They sent me to UVA, the closest hospital.

It scared us to death. We didn't have any idea what was happening. Or, that more things could happen. We thought rehab was the last step and hospitalizations were over.

I stayed two days. They tested a million things and found nothing.

Turns out, it was actually a very good sign that I was getting better.

The doctor explained, "His BP was probably super low before the accident." (Since I was in really good physical condition.) He continues, "Do you know what Lance Armstrong's sustained BP is? It is really really low. If you are in peak physical condition, you can have a super low BP."

He said we needed to watch it. It worked itself out. My body was returning to it's pre-strike self. My natural BP is consistently low.

Good to know .... back to Kluge I went.

***

I did not like watching Jonathan's therapies.

He tried so hard to do all they asked. I could see the strain in every body and facial movement. It was too hard to watch him pour everything into doing what used to be so easy.

It broke my heart. The brother I grew up with, was once again having to relearn all the milestones we had long ago passed. I felt guilty; life was easier for me. I hated to see him work so hard just to walk, talk or use fine motor coordination.

Therapy was more than I could bear.

Chapter Fifteen

They Told Me

They Told Me

I asked early on ... They told me I'd been in an accident.

THE MEDICAL TEAM recommended my parents skirt the whole truth till I could handle the news. They were concerned depression may result complicating my progress. So many hurdles still needed crossing. Adding another, was not a wise choice.

The answer sufficed for a while.

About two weeks before I went home, after a day of rigorous therapy, I began crying in the bathroom. Moaning and groaning trying to get the words from my brain to my mouth, Dad finally understood what I was saying...

"What Happened to Me???"
"You've been in an accident, Jonathan," was his reply.

My parents knew it was time. They asked for a Psychiatrist to be present and tell me, hoping his experience would outweigh theirs and deliver the horrible news in a less traumatic way. Both my parents wanted to be there — this was midweek — they decided it couldn't wait any longer.

The next day the Psychiatrist came and with my Dad explained about the lightening strike. Then, the hardest information of all — my friend, Cole, died in the strike.

I Survived!!! He Died!!!

To be honest, my emotions were abnormal at this point; I'm not sure I responded appropriately. I was very relieved and content to know the truth about the accident. I didn't quite know how to process a Lightening Strike or that Cole died.

A few days before the strike, I watched the movie, Benjamin Button. In the movie, there's a guy who was struck by lightning. He did all of these crazy things: tending the cow, reading the newspaper, etc. It was funny to me. Those thoughts were in my head and trying to process that I had been struck by lightning was hard and confusing. What did it mean?

I don't think it took too long for reality to sink in. I began to question and mourn.

Why ME?
Why did I live and he died?
It haunted me; still haunts me. Why not both of us? We were baseball buddies, teammates, comrades ....
we fought to win, every game.
What? He's dead? Gone?

Wow, that was a lot to digest for an eleven year old. I missed his funeral. I should have been there. As my parents sat vigil in hospitals and rehabs, his parents went to funeral homes and cemeteries. My heart broke for them, especially his Dad, my coach. I should've been there to support them, as I'm sure the rest of the team was.

How do I process this information? The first person my age I knew who died. We both were in the same accident with totally different outcomes.

I grieved for my friend I would never see again. Never play catch again. Never cheer for again. Never share victories or defeats.

I don't remember if I cried.

SHOCK took over!

I cried and have cried for Cole many many times since.

I began, eventually, experiencing Survivor's Guilt.

"It should have been me, not him." "What is the purpose for me surviving and not Cole?"

I felt I owed him and his family something for surviving. What? How?

I got the better outcome. Surely, I should somehow give back to them for their loss.

I don't know if in that moment I flashed back to the accident … I have a million times since.

> *What if I hadn't been so restless and impetuous? What if I had just listened to the warning and waited? Why didn't I take it seriously? Maybe, I could have prevented the accident? I should have prevented the accident! Both our families would have healthy children!*

Am I to blame? Does Cole's family blame me? Does my family blame me? Do I blame me?

These questions plagued me. They still surface now and then. As an adult, I realize, I was just a boy who loved baseball and also loved his friend. I could not possibly be held responsible for the weather or the rare occurrence of a "Bolt from the Blue". But, the nagging sinking feeling of grief and loss will always be part of me and my story, a little for myself, but mostly for Cole!

My life was dramatically altered in a flash; I live with that. In the same flash, Cole's life ended; I've had to find a way to live with that too.

Actually, I live not just "with it," I live "for it"! I often think, "This is for you Cole." In hundreds of different scenarios, I feel I live for both of us. I carry him with me. Sometimes, I talk to him. Sometime, I feel his spirit near me. Many times, I think of his brother and parents and hope they'll be proud of what I am doing with my restored life.

I can't answer life's hardest questions like, "Why Me?" Because it was me, I can live to honor Cole's memory: use what I have to … help others, show kindness, make a difference around me, be the best I can be, etc. because he wasn't granted this opportunity.

Cole and I share a bond beyond this world. We experienced together what few have or ever will. I hope he and his family appreciate what I do with what I've been given … earthly life after death.

The day they told me ... changed me forever!

Cole's passing didn't allow me to stay focused on me and my inabilities. There are worse things, I knew firsthand. I don't believe death is the worst thing; I believe we have a soul and eternal life beyond this one, a perfect life. I am thankful to live more years surrounded by the people I love and who love me. The ability to make a difference in this world and share my story to bring hope to others.

I don't focus on the ***"Why"*** so much any more. I focus on the ***"What now?"*** "What am I to do with what I've been given!"

Thank you, Cole, for giving me this gift!

I am changed forever by your presence in my life. I miss you.

***

Note from Mom

I have Survivor's Guilt too.

I felt and still feel horrible for Cole's family! I can so easily put myself in his mother's shoes. Jonathan was gone for 43 minutes ... It was the worst heartbreak a mother can experience. We had different outcomes. I imagine to Cole's Mom that totally outweighs our shared experience; to me, I was there to.

Now, I get to experience life again with Jonathan, which is mixed with feelings of loss and grief for Cole and his family. I carry it too, like Jonathan and the rest of our family. We are helpless to change any of it, but the guilt still creeps in, at times.

For a long time, I couldn't see a rescue squad or fire truck without crying in the car... it took me right back to that baseball field and lightening strike .... I don't think about Jonathan without thinking of Cole. Seeing a funeral procession triggers me ... I know we are celebrating life while Cole's family is not. My heart hurts and grieves.

Every June 3rd is a bittersweet day. I am totally conflicted. *While I celebrate, Cole's Mom grieves.* So much of me grieves with her. I am so sorry for her loss, their loss.

Life is very hard with few easy answers.

***

Beyond the Story:

Survivor's Guilt is something people experience when they've survived a life-threatening situation and others have not. It is commonly seen among Holocaust survivors, war veterans, lung-transplant recipients, airplane-crash survivors, and those who have lived through natural disasters such as earthquakes, fires, tornadoes, and floods.

In her blog, Nancy Sherman, Ph.D., describes the phenomenon by saying that survivor's guilt begins with an endless loop of "counterfactual thoughts that you could have or should have done otherwise, though in fact you did nothing wrong."

In truth, it's not logical for someone to feel responsible for another person's fate, but guilt is not something we necessarily have any control over. However, survivor's guilt is a normal response to loss. Not everyone experiences this type of guilt, but it's often a feeling that is difficult to shake.

Here are some coping tips if you or someone you know is experiencing survivor's guilt:

- Give yourself time to grieve.

- Consider thinking about who was really responsible, if anyone.

- Remember to take care of yourself physically and psychologically.

- Think about what those who are close to you are feeling about the situation.

- Remind yourself that you were given the gift of survival and feel good about it.

- Try to be of service to someone or something.

- Remind yourself that you're not alone.

- Be patient.

- Share your feelings with those you trust.

- Try to stick to a daily routine.

- Consider journaling your feelings.

- Get professional help, as needed.

(Taken from Psychology Today website.)

Chapter Sixteen

Rewards & Challenges

Dad's Notes

FOR A PATIENT TO BE DISCHARGED HOME, the primary care giver had to prove they could handle it.

I was told I had to plan and implement an outing with Jonathan. While I implemented the plan, they would observe and take notes. If they thought Jonathan was in any way compromised, he could not be discharged.

Jonathan thought this trip was a reward for his perseverance.

They didn't prep me or give me a list to follow. I had to think ahead and anticipate every need for Jonathan: medicine, water, bathroom, handicap accessibility, meal .... everything!

Jonathan chose a fishing trip. He did not know I was the one planning. He thought I was going along.

I had to gather supplies, think about transportation, his needs: dress him, decide time (hopefully taking into consideration his meals and meds), take him to the restroom before leaving (if he needed, take him while we were out), get him in the car, drive my car, etc.... Everything was on me, flying solo. Getting him out of the car, down to the pond, fishing rod, bait, etc. — the whole experience was mine to execute. The observer was not there to make suggestions. Only to see how I handled every and any situation with a handicap child.

It was a bit stressful, but I was confident after living in rehab with him for two months. Jonathan thought it was a fun reward for his hard work in rehab. He had no idea I was being tested for his release.

It was an awakening trip.

I got a clue what life would look like, especially if we didn't see further progress. We never took for granted the fact that progress would at some point cease and be the place where we all stayed for the rest of Jonathan's life.

We caught a lot of fish; 14-18 inch Bass. I knew what bait to use! The worker was impressed. She had been there many times and never seen that size fish get pulled out!

Thank goodness, I passed my rehab test! It was an exhausting two hours!

Thank God, Jonathan saw more progress in his functioning and abilities.

***

Moving Forward ... My Next Step

Passing the "excursion" test paved the way for a visit home ... a weekend visit!!
The thought of it thrilled every part of me!

I arrived to balloons on the mailbox and Welcome Home signs on the sidewalk. Two families closest to us were there to greet me. Their children were my closest friends.

I was so happy to see all of them. I was most happy to see my cat, Pepper. He jumped in my lap and I cried. I asked my Mom about him a lot. I missed him so much and feared he would forget me. He instantly knew who I was. It was a glorious reunion for me. If he was the only thing I saw or did all weekend, it would have been more than enough. We loved each other.

I was gone so long, everything seemed new. I saw through different eyes. I hadn't thought about some things for so long they seemed new, like I was seeing them for the first time. So much distance between then and now. Maybe another lifetime.

At Kluge, I didn't think about going home too much. Rehab was my life. I focused on the work more than being somewhere else. I didn't picture myself at home anymore; I pictured myself in the hospital. That became my life. I suppose I adapted because I knew I needed to be there. I didn't question it.

Just before school starts each year, our school holds a pep rally. My weekend visit coincided with this event. I went in my wheelchair. I know I stood to throw a ball at the dunk tank, but I don't recall if I walked at all. I tired so easily. My friends pushed me around and we "hung out". It was the start of Middle School and for a few moments, I felt somewhat normal again. At least, I was surrounded by friends.

I was different, I looked different, acted different, talked different (I wasn't talking much at all at this point, mostly shook my head), moved differently. People have asked me if I was embarrassed by my deficits. I can say with wholehearted confidence .... "NO, I was NOT!"

I was so happy and thankful to be alive, it did not occur to me to be embarrassed. In fact, I never remember feeling embarrassed by the changes the strike made. At times, I miss being the fastest or the athlete. I feel different at times, because my path took me places few can relate to. Everyone knows "fitting in" is important to teenagers; not to me ... being there was! I focused on the joy of being among my friends, even with the changes.

Saturday, my parents had a little Welcome Home party for me... A few neighbors and friends. It was short and sweet: I wore out quickly. I sat in the recliner and didn't try to talk. I soaked in the comfort of being home surrounded by people I loved and shared life with.

Cody, my neighbor and best friend, stayed over. We played Super Smash video game on the TV.

My own bed felt fabulous! I slept like a log. Once my head hit the pillow, I was gone. The peace and quiet were a luxury I hadn't experienced in months. I yearned to be here again. I was home again.

My parents, concerned for my safety, lined the dining room chairs up along side my bed, so I couldn't fall out. Mom put a mattress and slept on the floor next to me.

Sunday, we decided we would all go to church together. Since I had been on the prayer list for months, Father Riley told us he was going to announce my attendance. I was supposed to stand up.

This made me very nervous. For some odd reason, I thought people might "Boo" me. I can't explain those feelings except, my brain still got confused and didn't always process things normally. I didn't want him to announce me.

We sat in the handicap section to accommodate my wheelchair. Dad sat next to me. Mom, Jeromy and Christine sat in the pew behind. When Father Riley said my name, everybody clapped. I was on top of the world. I felt so supported and valued. Mom and Dad told me many times how many people were praying and inquiring about me, but it didn't sink in. This day demonstrated to me loud and clear. It was awesome. They were awesome.

Getting ready and attending church wore me out, but it was worth it. I rested the remainder of the day.

I knew Monday morning meant going back to rehab. I asked Dad Sunday evening, "Why do I have to go back?"

"Son, one more week, you can do it!"

One more week and I'd be home for good. I tasted, smelled and bathed in freedom all weekend. I couldn't wait for the bonds of rehab to be broken, finished and conquered. Nothing could stop me now.

I was homeward bound at the end of one more long week.

***

Dad's Notes

I wish I would have video taped this weekend. The simplest things like being reunited with his cat, Pepper brought tears! You could see how much he loved his cat, but also the importance of the moment. He asked about his cat all the time in the hospital. I wish I had thought ahead better and anticipated the poignant moments we experienced that weekend. They would be awesome to relive… all the small things mattered!

***

Mom's Notes:

We don't all remember every part of our family story with the same details. We have learned to accept that. Our individual brains hold onto details uniquely. Even though our experience was a collective one, we still have individual stories inside the larger one.

I remember this Sunday Service in my own way. I can admit some of the details might not be correct, but to me the most important part is how I felt — no one can take that away from me or alter it. It lives in my heart.

All of us went to church. Jonathan couldn't sit on the pew by himself, his bottom would hurt, so he sat on my lap. This was the first time since June 3rd we attended church as a family. As we prayed, my feelings flooded to the surface. Warmth and tingling cascaded down my body. I said to myself, *"We've got him back ... God blessed us and answered so many prayers."*

The prayers and confirmation I felt in the hospital chapel on day one, came full circle. I was living out the miracle in living color. Sitting in church with Jonathan on my lap; God heard my cry and sent my boy back to us.

This whole pilgrimage brought me closer to God. Jonathan, God's miraculous blessing, was smiling and loving being back at church.

Monday morning was hard, but the best was yet to come... Moving back home!

***

Dad's Hardest Moment ... Day 12

Probably my hardest day ... Jonathan was crying ... I was hugging him trying to make him feel better. He said something that stopped me in my tracks: I was too hard on my kids. One of the most agonizing things I'd ever heard; spoken from my boy. The boy who loved to give and tend people.

He said, as I was hugging him,

"Daddy, you're not a monster!"

I replied, *"I hope when you get older, you will know just how much, you, Mom, your brother and sister mean to me!"*

That was excruciating to hear; even harder to record in my notes.

Thinking back, my Dad was a disciplinarian, "hard on us". Raising our kids, I was the parent who towed the line. I assumed the role my father had, feeling it was my parental obligation. I was the one who stuck to what we said. Judy, as Mom, gave some space and allowances. I'd say, "make your yes's, yes and your no's, no.

I was a "hard butt".

"Daddy, you're squeezing too hard," my kids would say as I held their hands. My wife refused massages, she complained, *"It hurts too much."*

I didn't heed their reactions to my actions. That's just how I was. **I learned, they thought I was a big strong monster.** They mistook my actions for my heart.

I wish I found a better balance in physically showing them my affection and compassion.

Jonathan spoke these words out of compassion for me. He communicated that clearly and perfectly. Although his words were stinging and heartbreaking.

Times of trauma reveal a lot of things. I learned things I never wanted to. Jonathan was not the only one experiencing changes. We all were, in personal ways.

This day, I faced a gaping flaw in myself; a misinterpreted perception by the very ones I love the most.

I share this not to defend myself or for sympathy or rationalization.

I share it as hope.

Facing giants is better than ignoring them and being blindsided later.
I needed to face the reality of how my kids viewed me.

How could I improve as a person if I never admitted it? Sure, it was hurtful, it stung, but it was couched in love and compassion.

When filters are gone, you learn a lot of things, especially about yourself.
I was going through rehab with Jonathan in more than one way.

***

Preparing for Home ... Mom's Notes:

We were beyond ready for Jonathan to come home. We really had no concerns in large part due to Mark's knowledge of his care and routine.

To have us all at home would be a gift we longed, ached and prayed for!

Before Jonathan's trip home, there were certain safety issues, Mark had to address at home.

We purchased Jonathan a new recliner, knowing his time would be spent there. Mark put the basement door back on; it was unnecessary and cumbersome. We removed it years ago. The thought of Jonathan losing his balance while walking to the kitchen and by mega-odds ending up tumbling down the steps was a risk we couldn't take.

Mark also put Jonathan's mattress on the floor for maximum safety. We chose not to rail him in allowing for the biggest sense of freedom and independence we could.

We have a few exterior steps into our house. Mark either carried Jonathan up them, or one of us walked directly behind him. There were already railings in place. A ramp was not necessary. We counted on his strength improving. We could add things later if our progress stalled.

***

HOME GOAL: *Jonathan walks with walker assistance and a couple years of PT on an outpatient basis.*

Chapter Seventeen

100 Days

8/11/09

I left Kluge Children's Rehabilitation Hospital never to return as a patient!

100 Days since I was wheeled into Mary Washington Hospital via Ambulance Stretcher with no heartbeat and not breathing; legally dead for 43 minutes.

100 Days from Lightning Strike to Discharge!

My hopes were high. Home was a huge step in that direction.

Look Out World ... I'm Back!

Chapter Eighteen

Bolt to New Reality: Coming Home

Jonathan's Notes:

My dad said, "This Weekend, I get to become an Outpatient. I was so happy! This Friday I get to become an outpatient. So, I get to go HOME. I can't wait! Are you happy for me? I am really happy for me!"

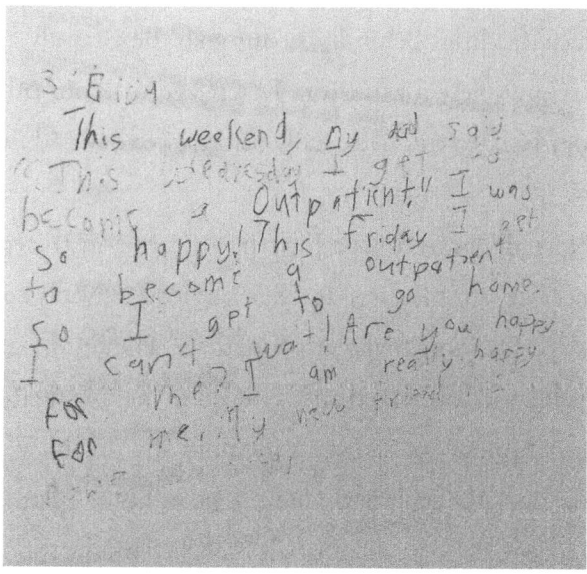

Seventy Eight days after entering Rehab, 100 days after getting struck, I was headed home!

I could not have been more excited. My freedom was at hand. I would live life beyond hospitals and constant medical care. I wanted to see friends, play video games, hang out, be in Middle School, talk about frivolous things, and grow up like all my friends. I knew I was behind; the lightning strike set me back. I was determined to catch up and be myself again.

It was a glorious ride home, knowing I would only return, to visit and reminisce.

I owe a lot to my care and therapists at Kluge. They prepared me well to leave and I was happy to!

***

Mom and Dad's Notes:

Leaving medical facilities behind was our goal. Be a family again behind closed doors. Care solely for our son. Re-engage with our other children; bring normalcy back to our lives. Exist under one roof and live life a little lower key.

We were eternally grateful for Jonathan's care and treatment; it was absolutely necessary for his survival. Even so, hospital walls held life at bay in so many ways. Our sole focus was Jonathan. The rest of our lives were laid aside. His life too was halted and reduced to making medical progress.

For months, "Home" was a distant memory and dream. Would we ever find normal again? Would Jonathan ever live at home again? Early on, it was too risky to think about. As rehab days clicked by, the thoughts seemed safer to entertain. We always believed he would return home, but standing at the reality was not the same. Twists and turns filled our 100 days; we had finally arrived at this day!

> *We were going home with Jonathan. Our hearts' greatest desire!*

We were ready in every sense of the word.

Everyone involved in our case was ecstatic and shocked at how far Jonathan had come.

We left rehab with definite deficits: Jonathan's gait and speech being the most obvious. Vomiting still prevalent. Plenty of work to be done from the home front.

We hit the homeland running. Scheduling PT, schoolwork, doctor appointments, and exercise needed to be included in our weekly therapy.

We slept by his bed several weeks. His legs were scarred with third degree burns. We didn't leave him alone in a room by himself. His speech was so halted and energy so low, we feared we wouldn't hear him if he needed us.

We used the wheelchair for longer walks. At home, Jonathan held our hands to ambulated instead of a walker. We helped with his shower, in a chair and handheld shower nozzle. He needed help dressing due to balance issues; everything was so tiring to him. We progressed over months to him finally becoming independent.

***

We came home to overwhelming community support.

Many friends and community acquaintances had kept up by email and Facebook updates; some we knew and others we didn't. We were reminded often that they were praying for us and Jonathan's recovery. They were a large part of our family's success and Jonathan's recovery; offering support when things were crumbling around us. Even when things were more stable.

One example: Jonathan wanted to continue swimming for exercise. We went to the most updated facility in town: American Family Fitness. Someone knew who we were and they would not let us pay. They granted us a year of free membership for pool time. We still don't know who to thank. Over and over again, people in our community stepped forward and blessed us.

Another example: Word was passed to us that a Physical Therapist wanted to work with Jonathan. When we followed up, it was a woman we knew from church. She had gotten her Doctorate degree in Physical Therapy and opened a clinic. She knew Jonathan prior to the accident and said, "I want to get him as close to 100% as I can." We think she did. Jonathan saw her three times a week at first, later he went to two and ended at one day a week, over a year and a half.

We tried to schedule his therapies in the morning. He was wiped out when he finished and needed the afternoon to rest.

If we didn't schedule everything just right; we were out at lunchtime. Jonathan and I (Dad) conducted a "Best Hot Dog in the 'Burg Competition." We'd find a Hot Dog retailer and rate the "dog" against all the others we'd tasted. We got a couple calories and had a little fun doing it.

We are happy to announce the winner of the ***"Best Hot Dog in the 'Burg Competition"*** is ... The Snack Shack at Spotsylvania Courthouse!

***

School

Christine and all of Jonathan's friends were starting Middle School.

Jonathan was not allowed to attend. He truly wasn't ready. He lacked strength and stamina. Still lacked major muscle control, due to severe atrophy. His balance needed significant work. He would get off balance; falling over at the brush of a feather. Anything caused him to tumble. Being with hundreds of other people in an enclosed area was an extreme safety hazard for him.

Speaking tired him. He mainly shook his head and used his eyes to communicate. He dozed a lot.

When he was ready to try school, a test had to be administered to determine his abilities and IEP requirements. Taking that test was a really hard day for Jonathan and the teacher. He could not help Jonathan and had to push him to finish. Part of the IEP assessment is observing how long and well they function. He had to finish even if it took all day. At times, Jonathan's head fell to the table he was so tired.

The instructor, "Do you need a minute?" But then, would turn right around and say, "it's time to start again."

When the test finally ended, the teacher showed great compassion for everything he had put Jonathan through. His stamina stunted a lot of his activity.

He was exhausted in no time. It was hard to watch; a daily struggle.

From that point on a teacher came to the house for school. Till everyone agreed he was ready to return to a school building.

Being home, everything seemed new to Jonathan. Being away so long and in a different environment, it was like he saw it for the first time. He forgot. The simplest things made him laugh.

Coming home gave Jonathan freedom. He couldn't do everything, but he felt it was his freedom to choose. A big big step.

He was on home turf; hearing the crowds roar, making plays and winning the game!

Chapter Nineteen

HOME

AN HOUR AND A HALF CAR RIDE LATER ... I was HOME ... For Good!

Months of physical and medical challenges were behind me. Here I was ... filled with emotion, gratitude, excitement, and exhaustion.

Driving up to the house brought things full circle.

The results of a terrible Lightning Storm took my life. God restored it. The results would be with me the rest of my life. My friend was gone. I had lots of work in front of me deciding what life looked like from here. Life had dramatically changed: ***a new Jonathan was emerging with echoes of the old.***

The time had come to start moving forward as the "Jonathan" I'd become. I wasn't exactly sure how, the next step was settling in at home and living as a family again... all under one roof!

Thank God for this gift. I knew He would see me through the days and years ahead. He'd already done the most miraculous thing I could think of ... he brought me from death to life, in every physical sense.

Very few will ever walk in my shoes. They are big shoes to fill, but I know God will be with me, always.

I am sure some things will once again become mundane, but I will still have the scars on my head, abdomen, leg and between my toes that visibly show the uniqueness of my journey, as well as the uniqueness of every breath and every heartbeat thumping in my chest.

I never want to get past these things. They hold the essence of life handed back to me from God.

***

Community Welcome Home

Please Join the Colson Family and Friends for a CELEBRATION of Jonathan's RECOVERY and HOMECOMING!
We are so excited to have him back home and wanted to share a time of celebration with all of you. Anyone and everyone touched by this incident and the miracle of Jonathan's recovery is welcome to attend. Food and fun will be provided. We look forward to having all of you there. This is a free event, but donations to the Colson Family are welcome.

Many community fund raisers had been done for me while I was hospitalized and many people contributed to a bank fund on my behalf. A website was set up for anyone who wanted to contribute for my hospital bills too. Plus all the cards, emails, and kind gestures done for us needed recognition. My parents and I wanted, very much, to thank our community in some way.

Our neighbor Beth, friend Linda and other volunteers offered to put this event together, before we even asked. They wanted to celebrate and encourage us even more. It was amazing.

A local radio station covered inviting the community to the event. It hit a few newspapers, a billboard at the mall read, "Welcome Home Jonathan"; it even showed up on the evening news. Hundreds of people came; it felt like 500, but Mom estimates about 150 people. We were overwhelmed and so very grateful. Mom and Dad gave verbal thanks to quite a few people giving a few trophies of thankfulness. The Sheriff's department came on stage and gave me a key to the city expressing how proud they were of me. My brother and sister were honored with trophies. Several other people spoke as well.

I remember a barrel ride train and a live band playing. We were asked to make a play list. Mostly, Christine told me what to write down. The only song I really wanted played was, "Rudolph the Red Nosed Reindeer" for some unknown odd reason. The Sheriff's Department demonstrated their dogs. Food was served too.

My Mom's boss, Mr. Thompson attended. He was like a grandfather. I knew him well. I'm told he and his wife came to MCV almost everyday till the doctor told them the trip was too much for them. When I was younger, he noticed I had a hard time sitting still. Mom explained, "When he's happy, he sort of rocks back and forth. He inherited the trait from me."

Apparently when sitting on the stage at my celebration, I began to rock in this familiar way. Mr. Thompson ran over to Mom and said, "Look he's rocking, he's rocking!" He and Mom had a moment of overwhelming emotion. They surmised I was happy. Mr. Thompson took it as a sign that I was returning to my pre-strike condition. It touched him deeply; he cared so much.

***

My church, St. Matthews, held a fund raiser shortly after I got home: a cowboy themed event, the Colson Dude Ranch. Pony rides, games, food and an auction were held.

I was still on meds. I remember slivers, bits and pieces. All the proceeds went to my medical bill fund. We saved what was left for any medical bills or therapy I might incur in the future.

***

Also, we started a Facebook Page ... Jonathan's Story. Other people's input really touched me and motivated me. I read every comment. I think they have no idea how a few simple words could aid in my healing; it did!

Our community was awesome and encouraging; a support to all of us.

We celebrated my recovery and their contribution!

I was ALIVE! CELEBRATING ... EXHILARATING!

Chapter Twenty

Reality

MORE HURDLES

My friends started Middle School. I couldn't.

My spirit wanted to, but my body couldn't. The rigor of a full day among lots of people with a load of academic and physical requirements was beyond my abilities.

I schooled at home on a reduced level. Many appointments and therapy requirements made for busy days; eight hours of school was impossible. Every afternoon, I rested — my body had a lot of healing to do. The doctors said, "two to three years" till I would find my full functioning capacity. I had a long way to go.

One day at a time was more than I could handle many days. Baby steps. Reasonable expectations. Short-term goals set my course for continued recovery.

It was hard not being part of the social activity. A people person at heart, I thrive in crowds. My sister claims I can get away with saying things other people can't... life of the party, class clown, quick wit, however you name it. I know my social skills and use them on any and every occasion!

***

6-18-14 ... Laughter

Nothing yet nothing is better than having the gift bestowed upon you by God to make people laugh. It makes me feel good when people laugh. It makes me feel accomplished like everything I do has a purpose. Laughter actually massages your internal organs! Laughter is the best medicine. Laughing can help you out of so many situations. Like when you're mad or sad or not feeling well or you are left to solve a problem. It might not help you solve a problem but it will definitely make you feel better! Laughter can reduce pain. Even when the pain is horrible. By the grace of God, friends and family, I've made it through pain. Laughter helped me through.

***

My Sweet Spot

The recliner; my sweet spot. My past, present and future-self languished there as much as possible. I couldn't do much on my own — playing video games was one. Family helped me with almost everything. Video games gave me independence. I didn't have to ask anyone anything. I had no limits; I could do it completely alone. My recliner, the throne to my compact kingdom.

When I was a kid playing baseball, I would try to run like Yoshy. After the strike, when I saw Mario jump in my video games, I would think, "I want to jump like that again"... it was motivating.

Christine, my nurse in the recliner, assisted me as much as she could! I didn't engage too much, even with my family ... it took energy. The recliner was prominent; a secure comfy throne to conduct my recovery.

Chapter Twenty-One

SIBLINGS

Mom's Notes

While life was consumed with Jonathan, we did the best we could with his two siblings. We're not sure, we did it the right way. Maybe there is no right way, when life throws such a huge trauma on your path. In hindsight, it's clear I see areas I would change: if I could replay the scenario. Safety and care were immediate priority.

We knew traveling back and forth to home from the hospital, a two hour trip, would mean Christine and Jeromy would be home by themselves a lot. Jeromy was fifteen, but couldn't drive nor be expected to keep a household running. We quickly decided they should go to family in Pennsylvania. We sent Jeromy to my brother's house, a place we've stayed many times. Christine went to Mark's brother's home; she knew them well, but had never stayed there.

Until this time, neither had spent the night away from me. It sounds crazy, but we'd never been apart. I felt the separation. I knew Jeromy could take care of himself, but Christine needed me and this was her twin brother.

They had never been separated for a night of their lives!

It was a tug of war, wanting to be with all of them. We knew camping out at the hospital wouldn't be healthy for anyone. We did the best we could. It added to the emotion of it all, but Jonathan needed us present for this concentrated time. We really felt we had no choice. We would have done it for any of our three.

We didn't want the kids to see Jonathan, yet. Things were unstable and unpredictable. I knew seeing him would breed questions we could not answer. Plus the sounds, actions, and scenes in the hospital were overwhelming, especially for children, looking at other sick children. We perceived it would be scary, frightening, and seeing Jonathan ... heartbreaking.

"Let's ride it out for a while and then, when he's more stable, introduce them to Jonathan's new world," was our decision.

***

Christine's Perspective (Twin Sister)

I should have told him not to go out on that field!
I didn't say anything!
I watched it happen.

I was born sassy; Jonathan winsome.

He probably wouldn't have listened, but I feel I would have won or we would have been arguing and no one would have been on the field when the lightening struck! I could have at least distracted him from going on the field.

Why didn't I use my sassiness/bossiness at the moment it would have mattered most? I think about it a lot.

Especially during bad storms. Jonathan will never understand that. I guess nobody will. I was the only family member watching it. I feel responsible ... I could have done something. I know I was just a kid, but I was the more mature one.

Mom asked me right before Jonathan went back onto the field, "Christine, go get Jonathan's Gatorade."

I retorted, "You can tell **him** to go get his **own** Gatorade."

After the strike, things changed.

"Can I see Jonathan?" I asked when I saw my parents.

"No, you're going to Pennsylvania," Dad said. I was shocked! Our family is in a crisis and they're sending us away!

All year, I want to go to PA to see our family; our annual summer vacation. This time, I'm being taken and don't want to go.

We stayed with our neighbor, Beth, one more night, waiting for relatives to come. I remember sleeping with the TV on that night to keep from being scared. I woke up in the middle of the night and some scary vampire movie was on ... didn't work too well.

The next day, our uncle came to pick us up. I think my parents wanted us in a different environment to get our minds off of Jonathan, distract us. I suppose it worked, somewhat. We had cousins to do things with. Our aunts and uncles tried to keep us busy. While there, I felt guilty 'cause Jonathan wasn't there. I was having more fun than him. I pictured him bored at the hospital. I had no concept he wasn't awake or cognizant of his surroundings.

I stayed with my Dad's brother. My Dad's side is not religious at all ...Uncle John insisted on taking me to church. That's what my parents would have done. It was very sweet and somewhat comforting, but I didn't know anyone and neither did he. I remember thinking it was so nice of him, but didn't really help me.

I was terribly homesick. Being towns apart, Jeromy and I met about once a week. I recall not wanting to do anything, or even shower. I suppose it was homesickness, worry for Jonathan, and probably general depression. Nothing made sense. Life was upside down. All kinds of feelings I'd never felt before filled me. I didn't know what to do with them. Everything was awkward and strange ... I kind of froze. I didn't know how to function in all the confusing strangeness.

"I hear you're not doing too well," I heard from the other end of the phone ... Dad.

"I'm not!!!"

"Well, you need to start taking care of yourself," he insisted.

"Ok, I will, but I'm not happy!" I told him about some of my struggles. I speak my mind, but couldn't say everything knowing everyone's life was abnormal. I pacified myself with food.

Jeromy went home after three weeks to attend summer school. I stayed longer. It made things worse for me!

I cried in the bathroom. Sometimes, I went to the bathroom just to cry. I never told anyone — never got emotional in front of anyone.

I'd never spent one night away from Jonathan or my parents since birth! It was really stressful and hard.

I stayed up until I fell asleep.

My dad would call my uncle to check on me, but often, I didn't speak to him. I didn't ask questions, they were busy. Mom texted me some; she learned to text while Jonathan was at MCV. I snuck away and called her once out of desperation. I wanted her to know what a hard time I was having.

The longer I stayed, the more frustrated, sad, and distant I felt. I wanted normal — my bed, my surroundings, my family.

Finally, after July 4th, my Mom's cousin brought me back home. I was so happy to be home, no matter what!

***

Mom's Notes ... Visit to MCV

My brother and his wife brought Jeromy back down for summer school. We requested Christine come too. It was time we all had a visit.

Especially, Jonathan. They needed to see his reality and he needed to hear their presence.

We tried to prepare them, but reality was far from their imaginings. They didn't expect to see Jonathan lying in a bed, unresponsive. We tried to acclimate them.

Neither asked questions. They pretty much just stared at him. I don't think they envisioned what they saw, despite our efforts. It did give them clarity.

Christine said few words; unusual for my vociferous daughter. "Hey Jonathan, it's Christine. I'm here and praying for you. I want you to get better. I want you to come home soon."

Jeromy held Jonathan's hand.

A psychiatrist wanted to talk with Jonathan's siblings. They desired to treat the whole family, which was kind, but I wanted the kids to talk to us. We didn't tell them everything, to protect them. I wasn't crazy about the idea of someone else deciding what they were told. The medical personnel encouraged me to let it happen. So, this visit, she took them for a bit. Her synopsis was that they were scared and concerned, but coping as well as could be expected.

The kids didn't really express what went on in the meeting. I don't think they liked talking to a stranger, but she was nice. They didn't visit again at MCV, so it didn't go any further.

Chapter Twenty-Two

Home ... According to Christine

Coming Home

I THOUGHT Jonathan coming home would be the end of all the "abnormal" and life would return to "normal"; pre-strike state.

I WAS WRONG.

Life would never be "normal" again. Jonathan couldn't do normal stuff. He isn't "back to normal." Our home life wasn't normal. All the trauma brought us to a new place; we'd never return again.

The first week was okay 'cause Jonathan was back home. We all were. Once again, we inhabited the home we knew.

After the first week, I realized, life looks different ... again!

My parents were occupied with Jonathan's care ... less time for me and I'm needed to help, as well. I missed my parents. They were doing the best they could. Honestly, I wanted more attention. In my young life, three months was a long time to feel like I had little parental focus. Now, it continued.

Resentment ensued.

Quite frankly, I acted like a brat!

After I saw how much help Jonathan needed, I got angry. I took it out on him. I said mean things. (My big mouth.) Our relationship was antagonistic. I was angry, which made him angry. True to my personality, I was relentlessly sarcastic. Sometimes, I was kidding, but life was serious. They didn't need my snide remarks and sarcasm. Most times, sarcasm was my outlet ... I meant it.

All my meanness led to punishment, levied by my parents; writing sentences in a notebook. "I will not call Jonathan stupid." At first it was 100 sentences, then 200, 500 and went all the way to 1,000 times. It took days. I could only come out of my bedroom for meals and the bathroom. I let them know ... writing these sentences would not stop me from calling Jonathan "stupid". *I was ever so charming.*

School starting helped quell the resentment and force me back into reality. I started school ... alone. For the first time in my life, Jonathan was not by my side. Starting Middle School was not an easy journey; navigating new building, lockers, schedules, teachers, administration, peers, etc., but Jonathan's absence made it worse.

I cried and begged Mom and Dad to let me stay home; "home-school me too." Lots of friends went to other schools. Jonathan made friends so easily. Not me. I missed his winsomeness. He would have thrived making new friends in a flash; I'd be tagging along with him. He wasn't there to lean on. I faced it alone. No built-in-lifetime-friend by my side or leading the way.

Missing him so much at school, highlighted how cruel I had been. ***I was riddled with remorse***. He had overcome huge obstacles with kindness and thoughtfulness. I reacted to my own selfish wishes by making his life miserable and being a brat. I felt so bad.

I started willingly helping him; becoming his protector. Appreciating, as much as I could at the time, all the work and effort he exerted to get this far. At times, I'd say, "I'll do it for you."

He'd refuse. "I should be able to do this," struggling with all his might to do simple things. He was determined to conquer managing his environment and becoming independent once again.

I suppose I became less self-focused and realized how much I loved him and needed him as part of my life.

*My life wasn't the same, but it had **Jonathan** in it!*

I went from being "Bratty" Christine back to "Sassy" Christine; I found my "normal" again.

Chapter Twenty-Three

Bolt from the Past: All. Hell. Broke. Loose.

Dad's Notes ... All. Hell. Broke. Loose.

I HAVE NEVER SEEN HER REACT SO STRONGLY BEFORE OR AFTER!
EVER!!!

When I saw how hurt she was, I knew I had done the wrong thing. Even though my heart told me it was the right thing, at the time.

I lied about discarding the bag, hiding it in a spot I was sure she would never find...

THIS DAY SHE DID!!!

A few months after being home, Judy was looking for something in the laundry room. She saw a brown shopping bag tucked way back underneath something. She didn't recognize it and pulled it out.

Opening the bag was like a demonic thing that creeped Judy out, to her core! Hysterics ensued; yelling incoherently. Moans, howling, anger, sorrow, madness, brokenness.

*The sight of them took Judy right back to **June 3, 2009** ... the most horrible gut-wrenching, heartbreaking day of her life.*

She told me to throw them out when given to us at the hospital, but I thought one day Jonathan would want to see them. They'd help him better understand the Lightning Strike.

I couldn't bear the thought of Judy being thrust into this doom ever again. I felt horrible that my actions had caused it this time. Immediately, I did as she asked, disposing of them where none of us would ever see them again!

The bag contained the shoes, socks and belt Jonathan was wearing when he was struck.

Truly, unless you saw them, you wouldn't believe it.

The belt buckle was melted to the belt. His shoes, were scorched and burnt, one shoe front completely blown off, missing. His socks were burnt, in spots as hard as plastic. The left one burnt more than the right, consistent with his wounds.

I've never seen Judy so hurt or angry. Believe me, I never wanted to be the cause of it! I felt like a terrible husband, extremely insensitive: gutted, ripped open, so very very sorry.

Today, we both regret disposing of them!

Time changes things... even the most horrible ones!

Chapter Twenty-Four

Bolt to the Middle

Middle School

NOT LONG AFTER I ARRIVED HOME, school started. Christine and I were beginning Middle School, 6th grade.

I spent most of my days sitting in the recliner, walking short distances, going to Physical Therapy and being exhausted. Wake up, Sit in a chair, walk with Dad, and sit back down. I progressed slowly.

School was out of the question; I was in no shape to maneuver any of it.

Christine started without me for the first time in our school career. We always had each other; walked to the bus, rode the bus, navigated new teachers, classes, friends, schedules, lunch, etc. ... we faced it all together... we "twinned it."

This year, she went solo: new building, lockers, friends, schedules, bus driver, teachers. It felt strange, but I knew it was impossible for me. I know it was hard on her and she protested to be "homeschooled" like me.

My home teacher came a few days a week for a few hours. The other days, I did therapies. My stamina was low: exhaustion set in quickly!

In January, all the professionals agreed, I was ready to begin going back to school; half-days. Christine and I had every class together. Mom went with me the first week to assist with writing, etc. After that, everyone thought I could function with Christine's help alone. We left classes a few minutes early so we could get to the next class before the hallways were crowded.

A feather or puff of wind could topple me over. I teetered and swayed without reason. I was improving; but hallways filled with students were a recipe for disaster. Walking tired me. Half-days exhausted me, but I managed, with help, and welcomed afternoon naps.

My teachers and administration were very awesome. Our principal, Mr. Wolf, actually gave me my own table in the cafeteria to keep me out of congested areas. I could choose anyone to sit at my table everyday: a much needed boost to my socialization deficit and emotional health. People were so thoughtful and kind. I was well taken care of.

***

7th GRADE:

I went back to a normal school schedule and had a few classes with Christine, but not all.

Christine was my academic support. If I forgot things, or needed help, she was there, especially on the home front.

I decided to be on the TRACK Team!!
I was still in Physical Therapy.
I Lost. Every. Race.!

I told my therapist I was running track. She said, "You are!!" "What's the best place you came in?"

I responded, "The highest place I came in was third."

"THIRD!"

"I was only racing against two other people!!" Joint laughter erupted.

Almost two years past my accident, I joined the track team to become fast again. I didn't realize it, but I wasn't walking with my feet straight; my feet were pitched outward. I also ran tiptoed vs. heel to toe. I had to make conscious changes to what had become my normal gait to run better.

I was tired after school; talking still took effort. Track for me was about improving my running, not socializing or making friends. I was there to get better.

***

8th GRADE:

My brother went to College; life changes again.

I didn't do track. I decided to manage the Girls' Softball Team. I already knew all the girls on the Softball team; a twin-sister softball player helps with that. I was among friends, a comfortable place for me. I was involved.

1st Highlight: I went to the 8th grade Formal Dance, my first official date, with Clair. We went as a foursome with Christine and my neighbor, Cody.

Neither Claire nor I were rehearsed at dancing: I was willing to give it a shot. We danced with friends in groups all night. One slow dance sounded worth a try, but my date wasn't comfortable.

2nd Highlight: I was ecstatic over being inducted into the National Junior Honor Society. Downside; Christine wasn't accepted.

I enjoyed every moment possible. I involved myself in those around me and any event I could participate in. I was making new strides, finding a new way to the new Jonathan; improvements came.

***

"Obstacles" Essay by Jonathan, Age 13

Obstacles — no matter if it's having a crush on a girl for the first time or the death of a loved one. The only thing holding you back is fear. Like President Roosevelt said, "The only thing to fear is fear itself." Imagine there is a wall in front of you. All you need is a little confidence and you can find your way around any complicated puzzle. You can't imagine all of the "what if" thoughts because those thoughts usually give birth to fear. I know the event that happened to me is just an obstacle that I have to get around. I am in gratitude to my fantastic team of doctors, my supporting friends and family, and most of all God for letting me prosper through my obstacle . I know that I have been making excellent progress throughout my journey to find "the hole in the wall" such as being a member of the National Junior Honor Society, scoring a goal against 17-year-olds in soccer, achieving a 9th grade status in Fast Forward, and most recently in my 8th grade year have been upgraded from an IEP to a 504. Through my obstacle, I've learned there is no need to fear when God Is Near.

Chapter Twenty-Five

Reshaping the Bolt ... Moving Forward

Father Riley

After lots of Physical Therapy, 4-5 months after I was home, I was once more an altar boy. It was bittersweet; we learned Father Riley was being relocated to another Parrish. I am very blessed Father Riley was my priest during my accident. He went the extra mile to minister to my family and me. Not all priests try to bond with families. He did. He knew the kids and families. It was a huge milestone for our church. The last mass he conducted — I was serving.

Father Riley gave me a wooden bat. Not just any bat. It was his Dad's; a peanut vendor for the Red Sox. He tried out for the team and ended up playing for the Red Sox. Father gave me his Dad's old Jersey too. He asked us to record me returning to the batting cage and hitting a ball with his Dad's bat. To him, hitting with the wooden bat was the sound of baseball. I did use the bat for a newspaper interview, but I wasn't hitting baseballs ... I used tennis balls. The bat was heavy for me, tennis balls lighter. I suppose he was trying to encourage me to rejoin the game. Pretty sure he meant the game of baseball. I never have. I couldn't bring myself to it. Baseball held fear, hurt and trauma for me. It was "my game": I loved it, but I couldn't return. The lightning struck me out in more than one way. Getting back up to the plate did not entice me in any way. Ever again.

Before Father left, he took the altar boys to Nationals Field in Washington D.C. to see Pope Benedict the third preside over mass. I hadn't been home too long: I didn't completely equate the experience with who the Pope is.

My senses were dulled for quite awhile. I felt immature, baby-like. I did things because I was told to. I did not attach emotions to much. I thrived following my schedule. I didn't question. What I was told, I did.

Seeing the Pope holds tons of meaning to me, now. A lifetime experience, being in attendance while a Pope leads mass… the man God has chosen to lead the whole Catholic Church. Not many people get to do that.

I remember this — as we were walking back to our cars, Father Riley was walking with me, he said, "You know Jonathan, I want to talk to you. I am very proud of you. I'd like to give you something." He handed me a walking stick he named Maccabaeus (meaning hammer). At the top of the stick is a wooden hammer. He told me the walking stick was made out of a tree struck by lightning. He made it for me!

Father Riley always carried a walking stick. He hiked a lot and people knew him for his walking stick. We'd see him walking on the side of the road knowing from a distance it was him by the walking stick in his hand.

Our family still keeps in touch. We were so blessed to be in his Parish especially during the hardest part of our lives. His presence brought comfort. He left indelible marks on our spirits and hearts.

***

5-31-2014 ... Five Years Later

Today I went back to Kluge. I had mixed feelings. Last time I was there, I was broken. I couldn't talk, eat, drink, or walk; pretty much couldn't do anything. I was happy to be there, but it brought back the good and bad memories. The smell of the food made me queasy.

These times are behind me. I need to be happy with how good I'm doing now. You can't live in the past, but you also can't forget it. It's with you forever. The only way you can possibly change your past is by changing yourself in the future.

***

8-10-14

Doctors never thought I'd live, walk, talk or remember. **I am a walking miracle.** God is great. He really overcame all the odds just to see me here on earth again. That's all part of the plan God made for me! I'm going to make everyone so proud of me and they'll be proud just to know me. And the glory goes to God. He did this! With the help of everyone praying, he provided a miracle. And I'm so proud to say that miracle is me. I wouldn't be anyone else.

***

Dad's Notes:

God blessed Jonathan with his recovery; no one can deny that. What the medical professionals see with science, odds, and prognosis, doesn't match our reality now. When I reflect on that kind of stuff, thank God I didn't accept one ounce of what they explained to me.

In my medical innocence, I held every belief that Jonathan would be independent again. He would function like other 11 year olds and hold the same options my other children did in adulthood. Maybe God gave me that peace. Perhaps, I just didn't understand the odds we were against. I don't think the odds would have mattered; I held hope for my son.

Don't give up. Don't always accept what people tell you, even medical professionals. Keep trying till you've exhausted trying.

Through Jonathan's recovery, his attitude shaped his progress and energized his work ethic, "I've got to get through this: I've got things to do!"

Maybe his larger-than-life spirit and attitude fueled mine. We were going home. He would be independent again no matter how long it took. I was sure!

"Life is what you make it. A journey starts with a step."
God's nearness and love ... Inspirational and Empowering.

Chapter Twenty-Six

Living with the Bolt

I STARTED JOURNALING ... in High School.

One day I was in my room, bored: I decided to write.

I often feel very different than my friends. I put a ton of stress on myself. I don't want to be wrong. I want people to be comfortable around me. I worry if I say the right things or wrong things. I don't want to mess up. I assume the worst at times. Sometimes, I obsess; make myself crazy.

I tend to have a lot of anxiety, stress. Keeping myself calm can be a challenge.

Writing in my journal daily relieves some of my stress. It's become a tool to process, release stress and record my history.

I journal every night. I record the days events on some days; other days I choose a topic based on my activities or feelings. On people's birthdays, I write about them. Filling a page in a composition book is customary; spilling onto the back happens. If I'm not home, I journal on my phone and transfer it later.

These black and white covered stacks are highly private; and I ask my family to respect me in not touching them. I'm well over 500 days now.

I hope when I am 80 years old, I can look back and read about the kind of kid I was!

I had reservations about sharing entries in this book, but decided, if they can help someone relate or deal with something similar, then I should open wide my thoughts and feelings.

***

My High School years from journal snippets ...

Junior Year

3-8-14 ...Pam

I'm still blessed to have Pam in my life. She's always been there for me and I know she will continue. I feel so close to her. That's why we are best friends; she makes me feel like no one else does. She makes me feel extremely happy every time I get to talk to her. There's nothing I wouldn't do for Pam. It's like she is my second sister.

***

3-19-14 ... Live for God

No matter how much friends or family mean to me or how important they are; I have to live for God. My social problems consume me so much that I forget they are such a small portion of my life. There's a whole world out there and there is the vast and holy heaven. I just need to keep focused on why I'm on earth. It's to protect people I love and to be a warrior for God!

***

3-20-14 … Answers

I don't need any answers from God! I don't have to try to be myself. It's best when I don't try! I don't need to try to make friends remember me! Because they remember me being me and I don't need to try to be perfect. My flaws and imperfect qualities are just things that make me unique! I don't need to worry about anything! I have faith in God and that's all I need to live throughout life. I feel as if my eyes have been opened! I'm the best me there is. I don't need to try and be awesome, I am awesome! In the past, I thought life just brings pain. But life is what I make it to be. I'm so blessed to have friends like Claire to set me straight.

***

3-26-14 … Why different?

Why am I not the kind of kid I was before the accident? I was great at sports, got girls, and still made friends. But who am I to ask all of these questions!? Only God knows the answers. I always get so bogged down with all of the stuff that is wrong in my life. When in reality, my life is awesome. My life is as good as any others. I can accomplish anything with God on my side. I can show everyone how great I am.

***

4-29-14 ... Storm

I don't know what is different about the storm. But I'm scared. I feel myself trembling every time I hear the rain hitting the window. I feel bad for scaring my friend.

***

6-3-14 ... Cole

Today was my fifth anniversary since Cole and I were struck by lightning. It was such a blessing to have known him. He always knew what to say. He was a brilliant human being. As the season went on, our friendship blossomed. We were always partners in everything. Even something as small as playing catch! It was instant and we didn't have to ask each other we both knew. We were partners. He was such a blessing in my life. I know he touched other lives too. Cole always stood by me. When I was with him, I forgot all my cares. Just talking with him, he had such a great personality. Heaven got an awesome angel five years ago. I know he's up in heaven getting home runs out of the park. He was an inspiration to my life and I'll live on his legacy.

***

6-7-14 ... Swing

Today, I was home alone for the day. I brought out a baseball bat. I got bored so I started swinging it. Sometimes I want to play baseball again but other times I'm like heck "NO" and tell myself, "Do you remember getting hit the last time you played with this?" Something inside me just tells me to give it another shot. I just don't know if I should or not. When something hurts, you logically think not to go back to it. It works physically and emotionally. If I do something to myself and hurt myself, chances are I won't do it again. Like if I have a girlfriend and she cheats on me, I won't go back to her. I think much of this world just lacks common sense. Being able to think logically. I don't really feel anything right now; it's like my mind is trying to catch up on everything that's happened. It's weird.

***

7-5-14 ... Math

I got through math pretty early last year because Mrs. Newton liked me. Now I have some other lady and she definitely won't cut me slack. I have to tell her I was struck by lightning to cut me a little slack. I'm not trying to slack off. She just needs to go a little slower for me. I have a 504 plan at school. I don't learn as quickly because of brain damage. Plus it's an Advance Placement class so that makes it a lot harder.

***

7-19-14 ... Best Girl

Pam is my best friend even though she hasn't been in my classes since First grade. When I saw her for the first time, she blew me away and something in my mind snapped and said, OK, this is the girl! She wants to be best friends, nothing more. I get that but I can't fight this feeling. She has always been there for me; even when I was in the hospital, she visited me. I know there are other fish in the sea, but I can honestly say there's no one else quite like her.

7-24-14 … Reasons

Every person on this earth should know that they have a reason to be here. A purpose.

***

8-3-14 … Marriage

When I grow up, I'm going to be the best husband. I'm going to do so much providing for my family. I'm not going to care about myself and my own needs. My whole life from then on is going to be focused and doing work to see my wife and my kids happy. I want to be the best dad ever!

***

8-12-14

Every day is a blessing. That's why it's called it the present because every second we are alive is a gift. And only God decides when it's your time to leave. God has the power and strength. He knows all. God is good. He's so caring for his people.

***

8-13-14 … Heal

It sure takes a while to get healed in some places. God healed me through the doctors. It's easy to lose faith and give up on God. You can't do that though. When you have faith in God, he has faith in you. It can be a slow process or fast one. It all depends on what God's plan for you is. God has a different plan for every single one of us. Different obstacles to get through, different hoops to jump through; if you stay in God's plan for you, you'll reach full enjoyment and accomplishment in your life. Wondering may take you longer and longer to finish that path. If you take too long, you won't have time to accomplish everything you want to from life. God works many many miracles but he'll call everyone home some day. It's inevitable.

***

8-14-14 ... Conquering Frustration

Today, I did two things. Number one, I let frustration get the best of me. Number two, I conquered frustration. When I let frustration get the best of me, I did horribly. When I let frustration roll off of my chest and kept trying, I did it! Frustration is just an act of the devil. It consumes you and makes your life painful. But God crushes the devil and his works. When I let frustration get the best of me, I walk away from it and talk to God. My first attempt, I did it. It helped me conquer my frustration. That's the best. All I could think about was I got struck by lightning and made it through every obstacle put in my way. Winning this game is going to be a piece of cake. That kept me going.

***

8-26-14 ... Value

Money isn't the meaning of life. I can think of many things to put before money. Like God, family, friends. If all you have is money, your life will be miserable. If you make money and have God, family, and friends in your life, you know that's a good life. Money is good for many things. But greed is a very bad thing.

***

8-27-14 ... Selfless

Being selfless is a good thing. It's the opposite of being selfish. It's doing kind things for people and not expecting anything in return. Jesus was selfless. Even today, there are three people who are selfless. I try my best to be selfless. It just goes to show this earth is not all that bad. There's still some good in it. It's so easy to think that this world has so many bad people; you think God would destroy it. He even said in the Bible how he wouldn't destroy a town for 50, 40, 30, 20 or 10 bad people. That just says how much God loves us. He sees the evil in this world, but tolerates that evil for the good. No one can be God. No one could have that much forgiveness. I wouldn't be able to. I'd probably burst from anger at what this world has become.

***

9-8-14 ... Perspective

My life really isn't all that much harder compared to others. I always thought I had it so tough. Everyone else's life looks so easy. They would probably think life is hard and mine's easy. I'll never know because I'm not that person. I can't think about this too much or I give myself a headache. I wonder what it'd be like to see the world from another person's point of view. I always feel so lost in my thoughts and in my brain, when in all reality, others feel that way too.

***

9-9-14 ... Worse

Sometimes, I feel like "oh woe is me my life is so bad". I wonder why I was struck by lightning. Now I know why God chose me and it's thanks to a man named Nelly who is paralyzed from the shoulders down. He had paralysis that was wrong with him but he walked like that disability was a joke. He was so full of life. You could see how much he loved life. God chose Nelly and me because he knows it will never take advantage of us. Just because it happened doesn't mean our lives end. Seeing that video today about him showed me someone always has it worse. It reminded me of myself when I first got home, and it shows the power God has on people. Him and I could have given up huddled in a corner and died. But instead, we both prosper through life. God bless Nelly.

***

9-16-14 ... Comprehend

What's horrible is, I do the problems over again and still can't comprehend how I did it in the first place. It's like my brain is a sticky note. So many times, I need a tack to pin it to my brain, but the tack never sticks. It sucks, it really does. My solution is to keep trying to get it to stick. Tomorrow's a new day. Maybe tomorrow will be the day I finally get math.

It feels icky to be the only one in class who must ask questions to figure it out. I'm just definitely not like other kids in my class.

***

9-19-14 ... Cheer

Tonight, I was at the football game, and something happened. The students cheered "Colson". No one has ever cheered for me in HS. Tonight, I actually felt like an important part to the team (manager). At first, I couldn't believe they were saying my name. When I found out, I was so happy I jumped around. I have a lot of friends. They always know how to make me smile.

***

9-21-14 ... Cycle

Sleep is one of my most favorite things but after the lightning strike I never get good sleep. One of the strike's side effects is a sleep disorder. Maybe that's what I have. I can get 11 hours of sleep and still be tired. Some nights, I just fall in my bed and wait to fall asleep. I try to think of nothing but it doesn't seem to work. Mom says I get this from Papa. I wish I could also get his mathematics skills. I need some of those.

***

10-1-14 ... Prince

I just figured out today that a junior will be on the Homecoming Court: one guy and one girl will be the Prince and Princess. My sophomore year wasn't really all that fun; nothing really went on. Junior year seems to be better though, there's more to be excited about. It's crazy to think of myself as a Prince. I sure hope Pam is my Princess.

***

10-3-14 ... Princess

Pam got Princess and I did not get Prince. The night Pam said "yes" to Mike was the night after we talked about going to prom together. It made me so happy for her to say yes. I don't know if prom with her will ever happen. I don't think I ever even wanted a relationship. I just want to always be with her. I know she loves me and that she'll never stop. Just like I'll never stop loving her.

***

11-8-14 ... False

I always thought I'd be the first to get a girlfriend. I'll be the one to get my first kiss. I'd be the first to drive. It's amazing how life isn't what I expected it to be.

***

12-31-14

Life is an adventure — I just got to embrace that adventure.

***

1-17-15

We went to the movies and saw American Sniper. I can't imagine how you'd feel, if you'd killed 160 people. Enemy or not. You still got a check on your heart. I know it's not really my fault, but I have a lot of guilt about what happened to Cole.

***

1-22-15

Maccabeus. Father Riley gave me a map on a mission trip. He gave me, his likely most prized possession. Father Riley and I have always shared this bond. Maccabeus is in the Bible — his name means the hammer. I need to be strong and sturdy like Maccabeus in my life. Titanium is a strong thing but nothing is stronger than a hammer. Maccabeus, Father Riley gave to me as a staff; he used it as a walking stick. Mac is tall and the top of him is the hammer symbolizing the hammer in the Bible. Maccabeus was made from a tree that had been struck by lightning. Father Riley gave Mac to me. He has given me many holy things like a rosary made by nuns, a cross for my bedroom. Father Riley is one of the most honorable man on the planet. He actually reminds me of Jesus himself. I can just feel Jesus when I'm with him.

***

1-30-15

Today, Cory taught me this stress relieving sense of rapping. It's great to get your feelings out. You feel like you're invincible when you're writing. Like picking up a superstar. And it's great to see how you're really feeling. So you don't have to say who or what it's about; it makes me feel a lot better.

***

2-7-15

For the longest time, I wanted to be a physical therapist and then my cousin tells me I should get into psychiatry. I'm going to visit VCU today. I'm not entirely sure if that's what I want anymore. I want a job that will make me very happy. I want it to make me so happy that I forget it's even my job. I kind of need to rewrite my plan. But I know God will steer me in the right direction. Everything I have is because of Him. It's just amazing how God can provide billions of people on earth with their necessities. I never imagined the time would come to go to college but it's coming. I've got one and a half years to get my plan together. I trust God will provide me with that plan too. I can't get stressed out about my life or it will consume me.

***

2-17-15

Tomorrow is the start of another Lent. Lent's purpose is to remind us about what God did for us. The devil tempted Jesus for 40 days and 40 nights in a desert. Jesus didn't have any food or water and the devil didn't even care. All the devil wanted was for Jesus to give in to his hunger and thirst and accept temptation. But He prevailed like always. To make it a fraction of what Jesus gave up for us, we give something up for Lent. This year, I'm going to give up my phone. Not entirely, I have to have it for emergencies. So I can call my parents. The only contact is Mom, Dad, Jeromy and Christine. Last year, I gave up my video games. The only other thing I use more than video games is my phone. This year, I'm going to test myself harder: how much temptation can I resist?

***

2-20-15

Who in their right mind would actually want to cause harm to another? Taking it so far that you actually want to steal another person's life away ... I just don't understand it. There's a lot to fear in this world but your friends shouldn't have to be one of them. There's no worse crime to commit. People shouldn't have to be looking over their shoulders to see who is behind them. It breaks my heart to hear about murders. Stealing someone's life away. I can't imagine it. It's terrible.

***

2-23-15

I'm starting to wonder if my poetic words repel girls from me. I don't say them to be dopey. I say them for them to realize how great they are. Especially to me.

***

2-25-15

I read my testimony tonight at Salem Baptist Church. There is one girl I feel as though I've known before. Some people I feel as though I've known before. That's why I came on so strong to Candice. I guess I've made up memories with them. It's just that it would have been impossible for me to know her before tonight. I've never met her. For some reason, I feel as though I've met these people. It's weird. The eyes are the windows to the soul. That's when I feel as though I've met them, when I look into their eyes. Maybe I'm just a problem child. I think so hard about when I've met them but don't come up with anything. I'm just so lost in this world sometimes. I just go the way I think God would want me to go. I still can't shatter that feeling that I know them somehow.

***

3-2-15

Tomorrow is my one year anniversary of writing my thoughts wishes desires and hopes in this journal. I've been giving my 100% to write in this every night. I thought writing down my ambitions would make them come true. I've had a lot of nights writing about girls. But I still don't have much to show for that. This journal has been so helpful, but my own ambition still hasn't had any light shed on it. Yeah, I've heard that dreams can't tell the future. Maybe dreams are just a visual of your own ambitions. I do feel like a new man from writing in this. I just know God is testing my patience with this whole girl thing. He wants to ensure I'm not one of those b***

pigs who goes out with a girl just for the heck of it. I know God will show me, steer me in the right direction.

***

4-5-15

Jesus Christ has risen today, hallelujah! Easter is a day dedicated to the Lord. Even if some people try to make it something different. Easter excites me for eternal life in heaven. No matter how much candy that Easter Bunny may bring me, I will never forget that Jesus is the one true reason for Easter. I was honored to serve today next to my brothers, the Bouchard boys. I cannot thank God enough for the miracles he gave me. However, I deserve none of what I get. I am a sinner. But I have still have found light with the Lord. Sometimes, I disappoint him absolutely. But I always try to repeal Satan and his evilness. It's definitely not easy. Satan will try anything to bring you down. He's a lowly snake. And sometimes I fall to him but I renewed my promise with the Lord today that I rebuke Satan and his acts.

***

4-8-15

I'm really blessed to have a mom and a dad who care and love me. Just sometimes, their overprotectiveness drives me crazy. My mom and dad are two great people. They're two very smart people. Even though sometimes my dad wants to make himself out to look dumb. They didn't have four years of college but they've been able to provide a good life for their kids. It's hard to believe that soon I'm going to have to get a job just like them and provide for a family. I just hope I like the place I work or else I'll be complaining all the time. If I work somewhere I like, it will be more like having fun than doing work. I got to get out of the house more.

***

4-11-15

It has to be devastating to lose a friend, family or even a child. Maybe God calls people home so that more people believe in him.

***

4-12-15

Anger doesn't have to destroy; you can use anger to motivate you too.

***

4-17-15

By the grace of God, the courage awakened inside of me today.

***

4-21-15

Sometimes you got to think about the important stuff before extra things.

***

4-26-15

All my friends aren't true friends. I'm friends with a bunch of pretenders. I really thought they were all the realists I knew, but now… I wish they might be different, but I know what Emily Dickinson talked about in her poem, The Soul Chooses Its Own Society. There are only few if any people you can really trust. I'm not going to fall into an endless pit like my friends. They are weak and I am not! I don't know about them, but I know a lot more than I realized!

***

4-29-15 … Ever Since

Pam and Mike have been dating. Pam hasn't been the same way to me. I've always hoped Pam would be my girlfriend. We had such a long history together. I even saw her in heaven!

Pam will never know how much she means to me. She's one of the most influential people in my life. And even if we never ever get together, I will give my 100% to keep up with her. Sheh and I are best friends for life. Nothing can break the bond Pam and I have, not even Mike!

***

5-3-15

I don't care where I work. I don't care how much money I make. If I am happy, it is all that matters. Happiness is more important to me than anything. I never feel guilty about being associated with the workplace if I enjoy it. Nowadays, it's all about money. I'm smart so I should be a doctor, physician, or engineer. It doesn't matter if it's what I like! I might be there for my whole life. "I don't have to enjoy it" — that's crap. I should be able to work where I want to work not where my parents want me to work. I've got the drive to further my education. Money is great but can I really do something I hate? I don't know what I want to be when I grow up. But I want my mom and dad to accept my choice.

***

5-6-15 ... Lightning

Tonight, we were playing football against Caroline High School and I heard lightning. I got up and ran all the way to the locker room. It's crazy how you can be scared by something so much that you lose the ability to think. When I heard thunder, I just ran. I thought of Cole. I am living life for both of us. I love him like a brother. It was so great reminiscing about all the good times we had together on the baseball field. I really wish you could still be on the planet with me. If he were here it would be me and him. But now I'm living his legacy.

***

5-9-15

The right thing is always the most important thing to do. No matter what the cost doing what's right means more than getting away with something. My parents tried to teach me that when I was little and they succeeded. I want to be a man of God not one that has no rules, no morals, no visions. That I would always do the right thing. And push comes to shove, you have to show your integrity. Being a coward and running from your problems just isn't the way to go. So my friends are choosing that way throughout life, and I pray that they start to embark on God's path. Life is meant to be fun but you can't have too much fun or you'll get into trouble. And trouble is bad. Getting into trouble can ruin your whole life. Doing what is right and staying out of trouble shows integrity.

***

5-10-15

Whenever I'm sleeping with my bedroom door closed I always feel like demons are trying to get me, but I have God on my side. I firmly believe that there are angels among us. If that's true, then an angel counterpart must exist in the world too. Cole is my guardian angel and he's always with me to protect me. And there's something in this world he needs to protect me against. This topic intrigues me. It makes me believe more in a great conflict. Someday, the devil will arise from the shadows and demons will turn on the earth but we can count on God to stop the devil and send out his army of angels to fight. I want to help, and I hope God will let me join the army for the greater conflict. Judgment day is when God will determine everyone on earth, who goes to heaven.

***

Junior Prom

(Non-journal entry)

"I've always had a strong sense of who I was. I wasn't concerned with being popular, but very mindful of being nice, courageous, a leader and having an upright character.

Prom was disappointing. People were "dirty" dancing, bad dances. I did not want to dance like that. My friends said, "Come on, it's not bad, we have clothes on."

I replied, "I don't care, I don't want to dance like that." I wanted to dance in the sense God made dancing for, celebrating, joyous not sexual.

There was a girl in a wheelchair. They said, "Why don't you ask her to dance?" It made me feel sad. I would have been dancing with someone who was like I was once. It brought it all back, having someone push me in the chair. I couldn't … it made me reminisce about myself and made me so sad. It was overwhelming. It brought me right back to my prior situation. When I see commercials of people who've lost limbs and using toes to do things. I think it is awesome they are overcoming their obstacles and not letting shortcomings stop them. But, these images make me very sad; their injuries won't grow back, I could regain some function. I once saw a wounded soldier with spine problems shaking. That hit me hard; I was so saddened. He was stuck where I progressed. It sincerely makes me want to c ry.

I had to leave the gym, mid-dance, sit down and think. They had sympathy for the girl in the wheelchair; they probably asked 'cause they thought I was sweet and would kindly oblige. It instantly hit home and brought memories of struggling to hold myself up and walk. It knocked the wind out of me. I couldn't do it.

> They don't get it. That's ok. High Schoolers don't get a lot of stuff!

I know my perspective is different than just about everybody else in High School; ***one in a million!***

Chapter Twenty-Seven

Beyond the Bolt

Journal Entries ... Summer Prior and Senior Year

5-28-15

    This morning, I had a very strange dream: Pam and I were being chased and I found Cole. We found out who is trying to hurt us. Cole has never been in any of my dreams that I remember. It was a really odd dream. I hope it didn't mean anything. But who knows? Dreams possess a strength that humans just can't master. They're like portals to different visions of life. My mom said how I might have been with Pam in class and since my six-year anniversary is next week ... Who knows?

***

6-3-15

    Today is the sixth anniversary of my accident. I can't believe it's already that long a time. I couldn't ask for a better six years. Tonight, was the spring sports banquet. I texted Chelsea before the event — we haven't talked for a while. I always imagined Cole coming back. Like being in class and he randomly shows up and I stand up and hug him. I wish I could give him one hug. I miss him so much. I think about him every day. He was my brother. I hope he's looking down on me and smiling.

***

6-6-15 ... Me & Christine

Ever since my lightning strike, I've lost everything to Christine. I used to beat her at everything. But now she beats me. That's why I play video games so much, because it's my area of expertise. You can't beat me. Well I guess some people can beat me, but you know what I mean. A lot has changed since my lightning strike. I'm not as fast or as smart as I used to be. But it's not all bad; there's so much I've gained from it, so it's all balanced out. But there's a lot more of the good stuff to come. My lightning strike has made me into a better person. Tonight, my family, my friend and I went to see a movie. Avengers: Age of Ultron. It was a good movie. I really like the Marvel movies. They're taking the comments and turning them into real life. Someday, I want to make people happy the same way some movies make me happy.

***

6-7-15

Today I got to talk to by far the most influential person in my life, Father Riley. I miss him so much. Boy do I miss him here but that's selfish of me to want him in my life. He can be an influential person to other people as well as to me. We talked about the sports banquet and how it went. I told him I didn't win anything. And he replied, "I didn't either" and told me how he is with the nuns in New Mexico. He said one of them had a near death experience like me. Then he asked me, "Brother, may I bless you?"

I never thought that was a question. I told him, "Father, I would be honored." He blessed me over 5000 miles. It melts me. It makes me feel so happy to have a friend so far away. I wish he was here. I can't be selfish. He prays for me, and I pray/write back to him. I hope to be just like him. He's my hero. I have the idea of becoming a priest through him. But in the Catholic religion priests can't be married, but the only thing I want out of life is to be a good father. When I grow up, I'm still going to be a very devoted Catholic.

***

6-13-15

I had a horrible nightmare last night: Pam was murdered but I didn't know it. They left her in a cylinder-shaped package in the shed along with Mike. I asked my dad who is this, pointing at the package. He replied "Mike" and who is this, I asked, "Pam!"

"I guess they had to kill a girlfriend too," I replied. I'll never forget how painful it was in the dream. I repeated "NOOOOOO," as I fell to my knees screaming, "NOOOOO." It was absolutely horrifying. Pam's ghost was in our house and it was like a real person was there. I could touch her. Much like Thomas, in Jesus's words when he was a ghost after the resurrection. I looked at her and I hugged her and asked can I do something before you leave? I leaned in and I kissed her. It's indescribable but I actually felt it was on my lips. Much like I thought the pain in real life too. She even said I was a good kisser and that was the end of my dream. I think it's showing that no matter what, I can't stop protecting her. I can't live without her. I love her. She's the most important girl to me aside from family. It was like I died when she did. I felt my happiness just drained away. I must protect her; I need her.

***

6-14-15

I have anxiety. I'm always thinking about how others see me; sometimes it gets so bad that I have chest pains. That's why I just pray a lot and meditate to try and keep myself calm. I have a stress ball my physical therapist gave me. I don't use it all that much, but I need to start. Stress kills me. I stress about everything. I just always see the right and wrong case scenario's. Reason why I stress is to make the right scenario happen. There is no 100% end to stress and anxiety; all I can do is to try to keep myself calm.

***

6-30-15

Running is a great thing to do to clear your head. If there's something you don't want to think about... start running. This time I started running with a cross country team. I might even decide to be on the team. I'm running with them to be with Christine and my other friends.

***

7-10-15

I'm a firm believer that there are angels among us. There are certain people in our lives that are angels. People who touched your hearts are angels. I don't know if this is true, but I believe everyone I saw in heaven — Mom, Dad, Father Riley, Papa, and Pam — are angels. Papa most certainly since he's up with God as we speak. My dad was telling me a crazy story today about a woman being in a car accident and a priest asking the Fire Chief if he could go pray with the woman and he gave her anointing of the sick and put holy oil on her. She told the priest, once he was finished, that it looked like she was going to die. The woman said she needs people to pray for her. Right after the police left, the rescue squad got there with equipment to get her out of the car. She survived and made a full recovery. They had cameras everywhere to record the incident but when they played it back, they couldn't find the priest. The priest must've been an angel sent down from heaven to calm her down. Also forgot to mention that he also told the woman "Everything will be all right. God is an awesome God."

***

7-20-15

Ethan is Cole's brother. He had an article written about him in the newspaper. Because now he's really good at football and colleges are trying to get him to sign with them. There was one part where they talked about the accident. I always thought I had asked Cole's Dad if we could play catch on the field, but it turns out it was Cole who asked his Dad. I think I said "Don't worry Coach, we'll be all right." The article said that Ethan doesn't like to talk about it, especially going into details. That's highly understandable. He was with me in the enclosed room taking SATs. I didn't know who he was; I forgot his face. We ended up talking after the SAT about how much we dislike taking the SAT. Tonight, I told Mr. Sayers I couldn't do cross country. He asked why. I told him the football team: I'll be there for them as manager. He'll work around my schedule but I don't know yet.

***

7-22-15

Why doesn't anyone like me? Does my lightning strike scare them off?

***

7-30-15

Today I was sitting watching TV when Christine came home. I didn't expect Pam to come. I was really glad to see her. We talked for a while, and she left with Christine. I have strong feelings toward Pam, but I don't think she knows how special she is. I've told her 1 million times how special she is, especially to me. She'll find out when she gets older. When I fell down that mail shoot in heaven, she grabbed my foot and pulled me out of the darkness and back into the light. I think that's the reason why I always want to protect her. Pam is an angel in my life and I'll fight anybody who gets in my way of protecting her! There's a light in Pam: you just don't see random people in heaven. It's the people that mean the most to you. The people who drive you to get up in the morning. After family, Pam is the girl who means the most to me in the world. I feel as though it's my duty to help or keep her safe. Whatever troubles she finds, I'll be there to save her. Just as she was there to save me.

Senior Year

9-15-15

I do feel like I'm making documentation of my life like Anne Frank even though I'm not a Jew fleeing the country. Everyone remembers Anne Frank because of those journals. Maybe someday when I'm gone, someone will find my journals and read about me and my hardships, downfalls, achievements, faith in God and accident. Maybe reading about my struggles will help somebody get through theirs. I'm like a gardener, planting a seed. Someday they will grow into a harvest of vegetables. I feel like if my journals stay when I'm gone; I'll stay and live on through these journals.

***

9-25-15

I got picked for Homecoming Court! I can't believe it. I know I'm great but I didn't know I was three years great! I didn't know it till Mr. Schaefer said congrats to me and I said for "What?" That's when I figured it out.

***

9-28-15

It feels so good when you're overwhelmed or something to just do an angry cry. Not like tears or anything but yelling at the top of your lungs to unleash your agony.

***

9-29-15

I'm special all right. Special means different. I'm the most special person ever. I wish I could just look inside my heart to see if the love switch is off. Dad is my only solitude. My family too. No one else wants me.

***

9-30-15

I'm just not as interesting as other guys. I don't know if it is because of the lightning strike or what. I can't put my finger on it. I thought the lightning strike would have made girls like me more, but no dice.

***

10-12-15

No matter what others think, it doesn't matter because God is all that really matters. When others don't love you, God does. When others aren't proud of you, God is. When others aren't happy for you, God is. God forgives instantly. God is everyone's best friend. God is an awesome God. Great Yahweh, The Almighty, The Shepherd, The Humble Servant, The Giver of Life.

***

10-16-15

I won Homecoming King and Pam won Homecoming Queen. I'm so happy she won. It's crazy that two friends since kindergarten, won! It's like a movie. I'm very happy Pam and I are going to do the King/Queen dance. I hope I can make it really special for Pam; she is a very special Queen. To me especially. The only bad thing is I think Mike, Pam's boyfriend, wanted to be crowned King with her. He'll have to get over it. My dad told me that Pam's father even said we make a good couple. Can you imagine it? I can dream but there's no way that she'll break up with Mike. She likes him and he likes her. She deserves to be treated like a Queen. Tomorrow is the dance; I'm going to try and twirl her. I think I have dreamed about me and Pam winning since I lost "Prince" last year.

***

10-27-15

All these past few entries have been about me, myself and I. They should be more about Savior God Almighty. Sometimes I can be such a child. There I go again. I'm in almost every sentence these days. Yeah, my problems matter I need to stop being so selfish. There's been some problems other people have that are probably 100 times my problems. I need to start thinking of others before myself; that's the next step into sending empathy. Empathy is basically putting yourself into another person's shoes. Jesus is the prime example of this.

Chapter Twenty-Eight

The Ponytail

That beautiful ponytail: brown, long, simple curls and sways!

I know it sounds strange and weird for me to attach a word like "beautiful" to a knot of hair hanging down from someone's head. It's a bit mystical, leaning on stalker-ish. From the moment my second after-death happening began, it captured my attention. I would say, it imprinted in my brain. I can't unsee it or unattach the word beautiful to it. The words tumble out together.

I know in those "dream, after-life" movies; it was vitally significant!

In that reality, it brought me comfort, "homeness", and security. An image of a safe person, someone I trusted beyond the moment. She brought me peace, stability, and compassion in terrifying times.

She literally snatched me from darkness. I was headed into a hole of black and she jerked me back from death, is how I see it.

She saved me!

When I woke, the memory was prominent. I didn't have to think about it. It was part of me like every other memory I had before the strike. The details were vivid, easily accessible. The scene was dramatic, but the ponytail preeminent.

I never saw her face, but purity and light emanated from her. I would do anything to help her or save her, as she did me.

After I returned home and started seeing people again, it slowly dawned on me …

That ponytail was Pam's.

The girl I met and "married" in Kindergarten! The girl I spent recess and class time with through Kindergarten and First Grade.

Once I saw it, I couldn't unsee it! Her hair hung the same, same color, same sways. There it was … that was it! The same ponytail I saw beyond, became real again in life after the strike.

If Father Riley appeared in my after-life/coma days, another real person in my earthly life, why couldn't this nurse with the ponytail be in my real life too?

She saved me! Pam saved me!

Those were my exact feelings and thoughts, when the person connected to the ponytail was revealed to my consciousness. How could I repay her? Do I tell her? Would she ever understand her significance to me? Was I crazy? Should I tell anyone?

A whole new level of questions and thoughts swirled around me.

We were young teens, middle schoolers. Who says these kinds of things? How do you say them? No one I knew had been through anything similar to consult!

I had to tell her!

I drew a picture of the conveyor belt memory. I tried to explain in a simple way that she was very very important to me and was part of my after-life experience. I think she didn't know how to respond.

How would I respond, if I hadn't experienced it?

It didn't seem a big deal to her.
It was a HUGE deal to me ... she rescued me ... SAVED my life!

She's the reason I'm alive, back, not buried in a grave somewhere!

I was falling to my death and she grabbed me, bringing me back!
Doesn't she get the significance of that? It is as real to me as breathing, waking, living.
I think to her, it was a dream. As hard as I tried to transfer the experience to her, it didn't. Maybe it was creepy or scary. She didn't verbalize.
Of course, I wanted it to click with her, trigger something. I wanted her to understand what I'd been through more than others, cause she was

there. It didn't! None of that happened despite my deepest desires for it to be so. I wished my telling her brought back a memory to her or somehow connected her subconscious to the truth of it. It went no where.

It may have made me weirder, stranger. I was already the "lightning boy." Let's add something else to the pot. Put it all out there!

I don't regret telling her, but the results weren't as I hoped. I still don't think she understands.

***

Pam Now

We've remained friends, sometimes closer than others. I will always want to protect her, care for her, and repay her. I have no choice. My natural inclinations take over and my whole heart and soul want to keep her from harm or disastrous results, as she did me.

She had a boyfriend in High School into College; I thought he was a nice guy, but I didn't feel he treated her right. As time went on, I noticed it more. I felt totally defensive for her and was so sad to see her mistreated. I can barely contain my thoughts over things like this concerning her. I want people to appreciate her like I do! I want to "save" her from bad things, unhealthy relationships.

It wells up in me as a "must" not just a "would like to."

I will always care about Pam! I will always want to protect her and give back to her. I will always consider her a huge part of my recovery. I would drop anything at a moment's notice to assist her.

Putting the "ponytail" piece together in my story was an awesome moment for me. It didn't look like the same ponytail. With every fiber of my being, I am convinced, it **WAS** the same ponytail.

Pam was part of my post-strike life. I was either dead in the afterlife, or comatose. I can't begin to explain it, but it's as real as anything in my life. It happened to me, like the "Lady in the Red", Father Riley, and seeing my Poppa!

You don't have to believe it .... I KNOW it's true!

Chapter Twenty-Nine

Bolt Revisions ... Life Changes

***I remember going to the baseball field that day* and being with the players when they called "Delay of game."**

The Doctors told me that maybe someday I will see the whole scenario play out in a dream. It happened to other patients who've had similar experiences. So far, it hasn't.

My last real memory before the strike is waiting in the parking lot during the delay. I don't even remember Cole being there. He came late and missed part of the game; he forgot his cleats and went back home to get them. I don't remember him returning.

I don't remember going back on the field or even us asking to go throw the baseball.

I've read and heard accounts, so I can mesh that into my memories, but I honestly don't have those memories.

Baseball was MY game. I never considered going back. I didn't want to! I suppose the hurt was too deep. The trauma won't let me.

***

Biggest Change

To me my biggest change, is my appearance. When I look in the mirror, I don't see the person I see in my childhood pictures.

When I got home from rehab, I looked at an Easter picture and I looked nothing like the boy in the picture. My face looked chubbier. I didn't feel like that boy. I don't feel the same. The strike altered the outside and inside of me. The picture felt like someone else.

It's more than age, more dramatic. I resemble that boy but when I got home, my growth and maturing started over again. I went back to square one — the strike took that boy away. Now, I am the boy after the strike. My life began over. I feel now I grew up as a "skin and bones, post-trauma kid." Not as the kid I see in that Easter picture.

The kid I saw at the rehab center is the boy I grew up from; the one with disabilities. Not the healthy boy in my young photos.

I know it's an internal thing. I do look like that boy. Inside of me, it doesn't feel like it's me ... I'm not the same person.

My rebirth after my death at the lightning strike somehow rebooted my self-image. I hold many of the same characteristics inside and out of "Jonathan before the strike." But, my self-image begins 43 minutes after the strike not from my physical birth.

***

I Wouldn't Go Back

The strike has become part of me, who I am. I wouldn't change it despite my losses. I've had many gains. I gained friends I would have never met: Therapists, Doctors, Nurses, Hospital personnel, patients, Emergency Technicians, News people, Community Figures and people who lived in my community I never met. I've had speaking opportunities at Medical Conferences, Schools and participated in Galas to benefit others.

Did I lose anything? Lots of people ask. Yes and No. I wonder, if I was never struck, how would I look? Would I have a girlfriend? Would I be the star of the football team? What could I have been?

BUT...

I don't want to be the person I could have been; I want to be the person I AM!

It took time to get this perspective. I've accepted who I am. That doesn't mean I don't have frustrations at times or wish I could do some things better, but I am at peace with Super-Charged me!

***

Biggest Family Change

I believe the biggest change post-accident is how we perceive God.

My Mom has always been a religious person; her faith seemed strengthened.

My Dad didn't show the same strength in his faith prior; his faith was strengthened and deepened, as well.

Christine and I are a lot more religious and serious about our faith since the strike.

We all believe that if people hadn't prayed for me — many people offering continuous prayers — I wouldn't be here. We believe the prayers fueled God and the result was my healing. It is possible God would have saved me, but I think the prayers made it better for me; I recovered more fully.

I am alive and functioning because God chose to do miracles in my life. It's part of me every day I live. Certainly, days have gotten ordinary and the newness of that is not always fresh on my mind.

***In reality: God is part of everyday I live, every breath, every heartbeat ...every* moment.**

Chapter Thirty

Epilogue

Christine

I am now 25.

I frame Jonathan's strike as a testing period — my personal strength and my family's strength. This time brought intense pain and growth in all of us.

I learned to be more self-reliant and to control my emotions/actions. It trained me to process my feelings, maturing me faster than my peers. "The Bolt" changed my outlook on life and shaped me socially and mentally.

I've forgiven myself for my "bratty" behavior walking through this journey. Being new to handling struggles, I went about it wrong, as many 11-year-olds would. I lashed out at my parents, who couldn't give me attention. I lashed out at Jonathan. I learned to take a step back before I move into action and potentially hurt others. I don't always have to be the main character. Supporting roles are okay too. My parents did the best they could in a foreign situation. They ensured my care and safety. Parents are normal people as much as we like to consider them superheros. They were deciding on the fly, trying their best. I'm thankful for my parents and how they helped all of us walk through this horrific time in our family.

> **I apologized to Jonathan during college, and he forgave me ... then I could forgive myself. I am very fortunate Jonathan was mature enough to forgive me when I asked. Our relationship has moved forward unhindered.**

After High School, I attended college playing softball. I majored in Recreation Management and Sports Studies. I have my master's degree in Sports Management.

Today, I am a High School marketing teacher with a goal of one day being Athletic Director.

I still fear lightning. I leave situations and go inside. Cautious about weather, I don't shower, bathe, or drive, if possible, when stormy weather is predicted. I consult radar not forecasts. It's one of my post-strike changes.

The strike enhanced my relationship with God. He helps me keep myself in check, my morals, standards, life balance, etc. He helps me process life. I enjoy praying and talking alone with God.

> **My overarching lesson: In the long run, family is one of the most important things in life.**

If any of you are the "bratty" sibling in a family crisis. I can relate. To you I say, "Give yourself grace!" It is all new to you too! It can be sorted out later when the crisis has subsided. You'll find your new normal, as I did. Forgiveness may need to be addressed, for your good. Please find a way to forgive yourself. It is paramount in walking forward with healthy relationships and worth it! Your supporting role is far more important than you realize. All five of us played a significant role in Jonathan's recovery. When it's all said and done, your family will need each other; that includes you!

***

Jonathan

Currently, I am 25 years old (2024); coming up on 15 years past the Bolt from the Blue that changed my entire life. A lot has happened since then. You might wonder where I've been and who I am.

After High School, I attended Germanna Community College. I worked at Food Lion Grocery store 4-5 days per week while I attended. I graduated with an associate degree in Science. I then attended VCU, Virginia Commonwealth University and graduated with a bachelor's degree in Health, Physical Education and Exercise Science.

Upon graduation, I worked at Hunter Holmes McGuire Medical Center in Richmond, Virginia in a research lab. We worked with patients who had spinal cord injuries conducting research using the Exoskeleton and Epidural Stimulation the goal being muscle stimulation and rejuvenation. As we administered therapy, we kept copious notes for research on amplification, stride length, and timed responses measuring changes and progress.

I enjoyed the research work, and it's link to my time of intense Physical Therapy. I quickly realized I could not become self-sustaining on the salary and lack of benefits.

My sister, Christine, began work as a teacher in the Public School System. Comparing notes with her exposed the differences in our pay and benefits.

After a year working in research, I considered teaching as a profession. I checked job openings near me. I interviewed for a Physical Education opening at a nearby High School. The principal informed me the position was filled, but offered me a teaching job in Special Ed. I'd be teaching Biology to students with learning disabilities.

I have my eyes on teaching other things outside of Special Ed, but I am happy with my position at present. I want to home in on my exact teaching goals and then move forward with attaining my Master's Degree. I can envision a career in teaching.

***

My Brain

Once you have a traumatic brain injury, you never get rid of it. Your brain is forever impacted. My noted deficits don't hold me back; I deal with them everyday. My fine motor functions in my hands are most notable; it's improved as much as possible. Emails take me longer because typing uses fine motor skills. I've learned to work around it and know it's just something I can't do as quickly as my peers. I've learned to manage and compensate for the bits and pieces from the strike that haven't resolved. I did not need special help in college although I did learn to accommodate in my personal habits like leaving more time for typing.

As I reflect on the strike, I reframe that part of my life as a very hard trying time for my whole family.

If I could turn back time, I wouldn't change anything!

I have met so many friends and good people; I treasure them. If the strike hadn't occurred, who's to say how things would have played out? Where I am now, my interests, my outlook would likely be totally different.

I am thrilled with my life!

The lightning strike played a crucial role in making me who I am.

I wear it as a badge of honor: I made it through. We made it through — my whole family, with God's constant care.

If I were to die now (again), I am happy with the life I lived. I wouldn't change it. I cherish the extraordinary miracles God performed in me. My heart is filled with gratitude. I enjoy talking about it and look back in a positive light. It walks with me every day!

My family was tested, in the worst possible way. Amidst the chaos, we got stronger. I am grateful and blessed our family stayed together. I realize that doesn't always happen. Again, that blessing is apparent to me every day.

***

Sports

I don't have the desire to play sports anymore. I go to the gym and pick up some basketball, but it's not a burning passion like in my young years. I accept the way I am; I'm not that boy anymore. I've found so many other positives in my life, I don't need it.

When I look at pre-strike athletic pictures, as I explained before, I don't feel like "that boy". My life started over at the Lightning Strike. When I glimpse a picture, my thought is ... "I would have been good friends with that boy!" We have a lot in common. I like him, but he is no longer me; I've made friends with him. He's part of my journey like a childhood friend. Our friendship survived into adulthood; I have love and affection for him, but he is not me. I am very much at peace with that!

***

Weather

In earlier days, I ran indoors with the threat of lightning. Not anymore! I am safe, but I will not allow lightning to hold me back from life. I function within safe parameters. I know the dangers. Yet, I am not glued to weather reports or even check them often. I suppose "strong willed" may describe me. Weather is not going to halt the life I've been given.

***

People

I am careful with new friendships, however. I don't announce my past upon meeting. I've learned some details should be left for later. Not everyone can handle traumatic information. Upon a casual meeting, I don't want people to know me as "the boy who died and rose to life again". Conversations are then centered on me and not natural. I want to be known for who I am today and liked for being caring, considerate, kind, thoughtful, etc. Who I've become and will become are most important to me now!

However, when I began teaching Special Ed Students, I told my story the first day of school. I wanted them to know I could relate to their struggles. I know about perseverance and dedication. Hopefully, my story motivates them in their own personal battles! I encourage them, "Don't give up!" "Accept yourself, flaws and all!" "Progress can be measured many ways!" I am the embodiment of perseverance with stories to back it up.

Many of my coworkers do not know my story. As relationships grow, I am sure it will surface.

***

God

My view of God and my relationship with Him, is the same as post-strike. I reflect and realize everything God has done for me, always. I see God as my friend but recognize His higher being. I try to better myself to be who God wants me to be. I make choices daily based on what God would want. God is supreme.

***

I hope my story has encouraged you. I share it to help all who struggle. We all do in some way. In the darkest moments, never underestimate what God can do.

My heart died for 43 minutes, no heartbeat detected, medically dead. In a miraculous moment, God commissioned it to beat again, and it did! Then he carried me, walked me, pushed me and held me through the impossible journey back to life and health. He'll do the same for you in your own unique life circumstances/struggles.

I would never doubt He could!

I am Living Proof!

APPENDIX

I. Photo Gallery

II. Crack Poem

III. About the Author

Chapter Thirty-One

Gallery

Fifth Grade Prior to Strike

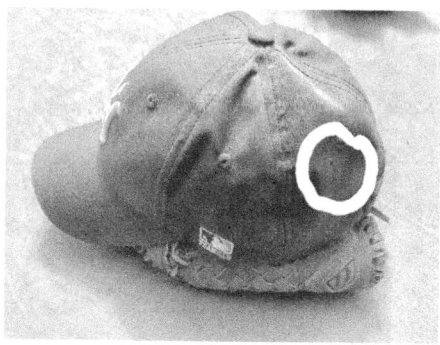

Hole left by lightning strike, inside white circle.

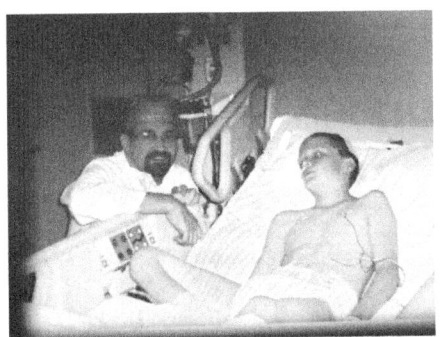

At MCV, when they woke me up from the coma. Dr. Tye.

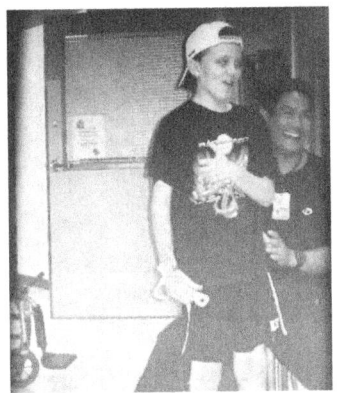

Physical Therapy, a few weeks in, playing Wii. Note my wheelchair and therapist, Brian, ready to support my stance.

A visit from my buddy, Cody, at Rehab.

Community Celebration.

Jonathan, Christine & Judy

A visit to VCU (now MCV) for 2009 VCU Children's Telethon: interviewed by Dr. Marinello.

Jonathan, Senior Homecoming King, with Christine.

Germanna Community College Graduation.

Jonathan 2024, Age 25

2024 ... 15 years since the Bolt From the Blue!

Chapter Thirty-Two

Crack!!!

... The Lightning Fell ...
"Call 911, two boys down" came the yell.
The prince of darkness danced with delight,
As day, suddenly became night.
The Shadowy figure sneered at the King,
Look at the havoc my power can bring.
Your people are helpless when I am near,
Their hearts are instantly frozen with fear.
They'll turn on you and curse your name,
And give You all the blame!!
Sternly the King answered His foe,
My children have strengths that you'll never know.
You think more highly of yourself than you ought.
You can do nothing without my will being sought.
See how they work to help those that fell,
Giving their all with their God-given skill,
And hear all the prayers being lifted to me,
mercy and healing their asking to see.
One life I've taken, his race is done,
The other one's journey has only begun.

My watchful eye remains on him.
As life is restored to every limb,
Doctors, Nurses, Parents, Family and Friends,
Faithfully serve, pray and wait while he mends.
Others are strangers the boy never knew,
Filled with compassion, they pray for him too.
The evil you brought has been turned into gold,
Uniting believers like nothing else could.
Satan, you think you've won, but you made a mistake,
True power is not found in destruction and hate,
Love is the measure of courage and strength,
To help another, love is willing to go to any length.

Written by Lavonne MacInturff
(Family Friend)

About the Author

Sass and non-conformity are ordinary for this Pastor's wife.

"Boxes" are for Amazon deliveries.

A nursing career morphed into writing; aligning with a love for God, families, and life. For ten years, Elaine generated a regional "reader favorite" *Family Values Column*. She has two nationally published short stories and a *Parent Life Magazine* article. Writing and teaching Bible Studies and speaking at women's events speckle her calendar as well.

Weekly, words fly from fingertips to internet on her Inspirational Blog, *Short Years, Long Days, Forever Moments*. Encouraging and inspiring in the peaks, valleys, and Tsunamis. Join the blog family at elainstone.net.

Lakeside living near Richmond, Virginia; her peaceful place. As "Mom" and "Zee Zee" ... Tada ... Mary Poppins. Beware of epic breakouts: dance parties and singalongs. Her Carrot Cake recipe; family secret.

Contact At: boltfromthebluebook@gmail.com

Made in the USA
Middletown, DE
08 October 2024